From Video Games to Real Life

From Video Games to Real Life

Tapping into Minecraft to Inspire Creativity and Learning in the Library

MARY L. GLENDENING

LIBRARIES UNLIMITED™

An Imprint of ABC-CLIO, LLC

Santa Barbara, California • Denver, Colorado

Library of Congress Cataloging-in-Publication Data

Names: Glendening, Mary L.
Title: From video games to real life : tapping into Minecraft to inspire creativity and learning in the library / Mary L. Glendening.
Description: Santa Barbara, CA : Libraries Unlimited, [2016] | Includes bibliographical references and index.
Identifiers: LCCN 2016029503 (print) | LCCN 2016036802 (ebook) | ISBN 9781440843785 (pbk : acid-free paper) | ISBN 9781440843792 (ebook)
Subjects: LCSH: Children's libraries—Activity programs. | Young adults' libraries— Activity programs. | Libraries—Special collections—Video games. | Minecraft (Game) | Video games in education. | Maker movement in education.
Classification: LCC Z718.3 .G58 2016 (print) | LCC Z718.3 (ebook) | DDC 027.62/5—dc23
LC record available at https://lccn.loc.gov/2016029503

ISBN: 978-1-4408-4378-5
EISBN: 978-1-4408-4379-2

20 19 18 17 16   1 2 3 4 5

This book is also available as an eBook.

Libraries Unlimited
An Imprint of ABC-CLIO, LLC

ABC-CLIO, LLC
130 Cremona Drive, P.O. Box 1911
Santa Barbara, California 93116-1911
www.abc-clio.com

This book is printed on acid-free paper (∞)

Manufactured in the United States of America

NOT AN OFFICIAL MINECRAFT PRODUCT. NOT APPROVED BY OR ASSOCIATED WITH MOJANG.

The publisher has done its best to make sure the instructions and/or recipes in this book are correct. However, users should apply judgment and experience when preparing recipes, especially parents and teachers working with young people. The publisher accepts no responsibility for the outcome of any recipe included in this volume and assumes no liability for, and is released by readers from, any injury or damage resulting from the strict adherence to, or deviation from, the directions and/or recipes herein. The publisher is not responsible for any reader's specific health or allergy needs that may require medical supervision or for any adverse reactions to the recipes contained in this book. All yields are approximations.

I would like to dedicate this book to my dear friend Ann Dougherty. Ann was an inspiration to those whose lives she touched. She was a cheerleader, friend, and inspiration.

I would also like to dedicate this to my husband Isaac, whose encouraging words and support kept me going through this project, and my son Jimmy, whose love of Minecraft inspired me to create the Minecraft in Real Life Club. He's taught me just about everything I know about the game.

Contents

Introduction

We live in a world dominated by screens. iPads are being given out to students at schools, smartphones are everywhere, and many people have a screen of some kind in just about every room of their house. Screens are so prevalent, even among very young children, that the American Academy of Pediatrics have recently changed their "no screens before age 2" and a limit of 2 hours a day for older children recommendations to a more practical approach that recognizes the amount of screens present in the lives of children at home and at school. According to a study conducted by Common Sense Media, tweens aged 8–12 years spend an average of about 4 ½ hours a day with screen media, and this is not inclusive of any time spent working on school-related tasks (Common Sense Media 2015). Even in the library, we struggle to find that balance between keeping up with technology and staying relevant, while still keeping to our core mission of literacy and education. Like parents, librarians are struggling with the idea of screen time and how to balance it in their work. At the same time, parents are looking to engage their kids in activities where screens are not the focus, and many of those parents are turning to libraries to provide this kind of activity.

So, what do you do and how do you walk the line between not enough technology and too much technology? How can you please those parents who are looking to limit their children's screen time with meeting the needs of families who may not have access to high-speed Internet and technology in their homes? Further, since most of this time spent with screens is as consumers rather than creators, when you bring screen time into your programs, how do you do it in a meaningful way?

This is where the activities presented in this book come in. What if you could tap into something that kids are fanatical about in a way that does not have to rely on technology? What if you could use this interest to engage learning in a meaningful but fun way? And, when you bring screens into the program, is the engagement as a creator rather than consumer? The open-ended nature of Minecraft and the love kids have for this game make it the perfect tool for bringing hands-on learning activities to your library that can introduce a variety of subjects in a fun way that develops 21st-century skills growing kids into creators rather than merely consumers.

Minecraft in Real Life is about using Minecraft as a jumping-off point to creating hands-on projects and activities, to engage young library users in learning and inspire their creativity. There has been much written about using Minecraft as a tool for learning, but many of these works focus on using in-game activities as the entry point to the learning experience. While there is nothing wrong with this approach, there are obstacles that many librarians face in bringing this kind of activity to the library. Some of us face opposition from library boards or administration that do not see the value of video games, never mind creating programming around gameplay. Others may face financial and technological obstacles that make offering a program reliant on computers and Internet connectivity out of the reach for their location. Lack of comfort with technology or not having the background necessary to set up a server is yet another obstacle standing in the way of bringing Minecraft gameplay to the library setting. While these may be obstacles that you can overcome, it can often be a difficult, slow, and time-consuming process. Why go down this path when there is another way to use Minecraft in the library that gets kids creating, thinking, and learning?

This book provides ideas for programs and activities that can be used in a variety of library settings. Many of the activities can be scaled to your setting, budget, and comfort level. While some of the activities are similar to things you may already do in your library, others will be new, introducing you to new areas of exploration and learning. As you grow your own skills and knowledge base, you can introduce more advanced activities to your group. If you find that many of the kids attend on a regular basis, they will also be growing their skills and looking to work on more advanced projects.

Before Minecraft in Real Life activities are introduced, take a look at the reasons why hands-on, project-based activities are a good fit not only for library programming, but also the benefits this type of programming offers. The opening chapters of this book take a brief look at the Maker Movement, 21st-century learning skills as they pertain particularly to the library setting, and why Minecraft is the perfect tool for building these skills. The following chapters describe a variety of activities from 3D printing to literacy activities to more traditional craft projects that you can easily implement in your library.

This book is really just the tip of the iceberg as to how Minecraft can be used to launch hands-on learning. I hope you will not only try out some of the activities presented here, but also that these activities allow you to see the possibilities and create your own unique Minecraft in Real Life projects.

1

Minecraft and the Maker Movement

A BRIEF LOOK AT MINECRAFT

What is it about Minecraft that has captured the imagination and attention of so many kids and even a lot of adults around the world? When Minecraft was created, no one imagined that it would take off to become one of the most popular games of all time. If you want to get an idea of just how popular Minecraft is, and this is just the PC edition, take a look at the statistics page at http://mojang.net/stats. As of June 2016, sales of the game are averaging 53,000 units *per day*. Minecraft grew from a little sandbox game on the PC to a virtual empire, selling over 100 million copies across all platforms, including PC, Xbox, PlayStation, Android, and iOS versions. In 2014, Microsoft acquired Minecraft for $2.5 billion! There were some who predicted that Microsoft's acquisition of the game meant that interest was waning and that people would no longer be interested in the game now that a big company bought it out, but by the looks of the amount of products, YouTube videos, and even Microsoft's plans for the game, that is not true. If anything, Minecraft is as popular as ever!

The popularity of Minecraft amongst today's youth is something that seems to confuse many parents. Why are kids so interested in a game that doesn't have flashy graphics and no real narrative? Sure, there are characters: you start the game as Steve or Alex and you encounter creatures along the way such as Creepers, Endermen, and Villagers, but even when playing in survival mode, there is no narrative guiding the game. The fact that there is no narrative is a big part of the appeal. In a world where much of the imagination is taken out of children's play, Minecraft offers a world of possibilities. When

Marcus "Notch" Persson was describing the game he was creating to his mother, who like so many parents today didn't really understand what he was trying to do, he told her how the game would be easily accessible but complicated at the same time (Linus n.d.).

You can think of Minecraft as LEGO before LEGO became about sets based around movies, TV shows, and even LEGO's own created worlds. LEGO could be described in the same way. It's easy to "learn" how to put LEGO together, but it's more difficult to learn how to build something that looks like something with them. If you walk into any Toys R' Us, Target, or a similar store, it's hard to find a box of LEGO bricks that are not attached to a set of some sort. It's funny when you think about the story being told in the LEGO movie, but this seems in many ways what LEGO has become, even for kids. They become about following directions to build a playset that is tied into a story that already exists, and while kids may make up their own stories around these properties, they are often tied to creating the narrative around Ninja Turtles, superheroes, or ninjas.

One of the more interesting things about Minecraft, and part of its appeal, is something that you don't find with many other video games. The creator of the game is a celebrity in his own right, and just about every kid knows the name of the designer as well as many of the people who were part of the Mojang Minecraft team prior to it being purchased by Microsoft. What Notch did with Minecraft was definitely a new approach and has changed gaming. While he makes no secret that Minecraft was inspired by another indie game called Infiniminer, by sharing the game as it was being created, he set into motion a new approach to game development. Of course, Minecraft may not be the first game to try this approach, but it certainly shaped and made this model popular. With Minecraft, you are no longer only a player of a final product developed by programmers and game designers, but part of a growing community that in turn helps shape the game. Players still eagerly await the next update, which brings new features, many of which are features that players have requested developers to add.

It is amazing to think that Minecraft, the most downloaded game of all time, was able to build its success without spending any money on advertising. Like the growth of YouTube celebrities, this was a game that grew virally, through word of mouth, fills a market niche that seems to elude traditional entertainment companies. The success and expectations of fans proved to be a lot of pressure for Notch, who did what he said he would never do when he sold the game to a big, mainstream corporation. While Notch was no longer interested in being burdened by the responsibility associated with this public persona, which attracted not only adulation, but also the nastier side of being a public persona in the age of Twitter, the game lives on and is branching out in new directions.

Minecraft can be thought of as digital building blocks. Blocks aren't high tech or fancy toys, but they continue to hold appeal for children even with all the other toys competing for attention on the toys shelves. It's often the simplest toys that have staying power because they hold the greatest possibilities for creativity and engagement. I think the same can be said for Minecraft.

There's a reason why it's called a sandbox game. In a sandbox, you can build and create using simple tools and materials. When you start the game, you can choose which mode to begin in, Creative or Survival. In Creative Mode, you are given all the tools and materials you need to start building and creating. You don't have to worry about creatures "killing" you, about eating to maintain your "health," or even worry about falling off a cliff. This is like dumping out a box of toy bricks and sitting on the floor creating. Your other choice is to start in Survival Mode where you have to gather supplies and resources in order to survive. The first challenge is usually to build a house or some kind of shelter to protect you against the creatures that come out at night such as the infamous Creeper. Now, you can control how difficult it is to survive in Survival Mode, though changing the settings. In Peaceful Mode, you still have to be careful about walking through lava or falling off a cliff, but there are no hostile mobs looking to destroy you. As you progress through the difficulty levels, there are more and more things that can hurt you, and you need to be cleverer in your construction in order to survive the hostile creatures looking for you. In Survival Mode, you are not given everything you need to survive; instead, you will need to harvest materials and craft what you need.

If you miss the stories that video games often weave, check out Minecraft Story Mode. Minecraft Story Mode was recently released by TellTale Games. Minecraft Story Mode is a bit like one of those Choose Your Own Adventure books. The story puts the player in control of the story, making decisions and taking actions that will affect the outcome of the story. The star of this story is Jesse, whom you can play as a boy or a girl, and choose the appearance of your character to look the most like you or not. The story centers around terror unleashed "Order of the Stone" and travel across the various Minecraft realms to save the world. The game will be the first version of Minecraft available on a Nintendo platform and is currently available for tablets, PC, Xbox, and

PlayStation consoles. An interesting feature is the way they are releasing the game. Instead of releasing as one complete game, it's coming out in chapters so that more of the complete story will be revealed as each chapter comes out.

THE MAKER MOVEMENT

So what is the Maker Movement, how does it relate to Minecraft, and why should librarians care? The Modern Maker Movement is a bit of return to making things, discovering how things work by taking things apart, and exploring new technologies. It's about getting your hands dirty and making something. Sometimes, things are made with technology incorporating Arduino microcontrollers or using a 3D printer, but these high-tech tools are not an essential part of making. Sewing, crafting, cooking can all be considered maker activities. Making is about a mind-set of learning by doing, fostering creativity, innovation, and entrepreneurship. The movement is about being creators rather than just consumers of things. Anyone can be a maker!

In "The Maker Mindset," Dale Dougherty talks about the origins of the Maker Movement in what he calls "experimental play." Makers don't just put things together, they take things apart, they play with technology to learn about it, and they put things back together in creative ways. They learn through playing and doing, which leads to new ideas and often times innovations (Dougherty n.d.). Because education has become a very serious business focused on "results" rather than the joy of learning something new, the Maker Movement, and libraries in particular, can bring back that joy of discovery and be places where maker education can come alive, as we are in the business of helping people discover answers, develop their passions, and open the gates to learning for oneself.

Since *MAKE:* magazine launched in 2005, there has been a growth in the number of makerspaces and even Maker Faires in communities around the globe. More and more libraries are creating spaces for making, whether in the form of formal makerspaces, FabLabs, or hackerspaces and pop-up spaces that can be stored in a cart or closet. There is much debate about their place in a library, and as libraries struggle with staying relevant in an ever-changing world, that debate is sure to continue. In Tony Wagner's book *Most Likely to Succeed: Preparing Our Kids for the Innovation Era*, he talks about schools and how they continue to prepare kids for a world that no longer exists. He states that the information era is over as information is available at the swipe of a screen. The world we need to prepare for now is not the one in which how or where to find information is the end goal; instead, we must prepare our kids for a world where they know what to do with that information. What will they do with the information once they have it? Libraries are a perfect place for this kind of creation space, as we are not bound to a curriculum or any particular agenda. Libraries are a space for the community to gather and use the resources available. We can provide not only the space to gather information, but a space to create something new with it whether it be the launch of a new business or a small toy that a child designed and printed out on a 3D printer.

While making was a popular activity for much of history, it took a backseat for a while. In the 1970s, places like Radio Shack were thriving, selling all kinds of kits, parts, and pieces to learn about electronics by creating and hacking. At some point, this curiosity about how things worked waned. It seems that as technology has become more and more an essential part of everyday life, people no longer wondered how it worked, they just cared that it worked. The constant upgrading of devices to the latest, fastest phone or computer has led to a glut of devices. The rise of the Maker Movement and making in general is a bit of a return to the days of looking inside things, learning how they work, and then creating something new. Lest one fears the introduction of 3D printing and the creation of more throwaway items, making focuses on creating things with a purpose, reusing, and rethinking the everyday. It is very much about taking what you have and creating something new.

FROM MINECRAFT TO MAKER

So, how does making relate to Minecraft and how can we use Minecraft to create Makers in our libraries? By bringing Minecraft out of the computer world and into the real world, you can take the first steps in creating Minecraft Makers in your library. There are many ways to take the game and use it in the library through hands-on projects and activities that encourage creativity, collaboration, and the development of hard and soft skills that will help them grow not only as makers, but also as doers. Maker programming puts kids in charge of their own learning and provides a variety of experiences that can help them develop their passions. Learning through doing is what making is about, and Minecraft opens the door to many opportunities.

Since making is not just about fancy equipment like 3D printers or all about electronics, there are multiple entry points into maker programming with Minecraft. Food and traditional craft programs can be placed under the banner of making, as well. Start small, grow your own skills, and expand from there. You don't have to have all the answers or a ton of knowledge to grow Minecraft Makers at your library. You don't even need to be a Minecraft expert or player to use Minecraft as a jumping-off point for hands-on learning in the library. There is a wealth of information out there about the game to help you get started and get the ideas flowing. Use all the resources at your disposal, especially the kids who are clamoring for Minecraft programs and books, who are using your library computers to watch their favorite YouTuber talk about Minecraft. Minecraft fans love to talk about the game as much as they like to play it, and they are your best source of information to get you started.

REFERENCES

Dougherty, Dale. n.d. "The Maker Mindset." https://llk.media.mit.edu/courses/readings/maker-mindset.pdf.
Linus, Daniel Goldberg. n.d. "Wired." *Wired.* www.wired.com/2013/11/minecraft-book.

2

Minecraft in Real Life Club

So why should you bring Minecraft programming to your library? Minecraft gives kids a world of endless possibilities, which is not only its appeal, but also what makes it so great to use in programming in the library. While libraries have really exploited the potential of in-gameplay to attract new users to their libraries, there is another world of possibilities for using the game as a gateway to hands-on activities of all kinds. Like Microsoft CEO Satya Nadella said, "Minecraft is a great tool to open the door to learning of all kinds" (Soper 2014). The passion kids have for all things Minecraft makes it a great vehicle for getting them into programs, and have them learning and creating in all kinds of ways.

Is your library looking to add maker or STEM programs? Is literacy, whether it be digital or more traditional literacy, more the direction you're looking to go? Whether playing the game or creating in the real world, Minecraft is a tool that can be harnessed to give kids experiences that many don't get in the classroom and the opportunity to develop 21st-century learning skills. Collaboration, teamwork, and trial and error are just some of the skills needed to be successful in today's world, and Minecraft in Real Life (IRL) programming is a great way to help kids develop these skills. Using Minecraft as the hook will get kids in the door and excited to come to the library. The programming possibilities are as big as the game itself!

MINECRAFT IN LIBRARIES

The world of play is changing as we move from more creative, hands-on play to using tablets and phones, and connectivity is becoming more and more prevalent and a huge part of the lives of today's children.

While this isn't necessarily a bad thing, it's something that often concerns parents, teachers, and librarians. Technology has exploded, but our ability to keep up and find meaningful ways to use that technology is often lagging behind. While schools and libraries are looking to find ways to bring technologies into their spaces, it seems that many parents are looking for ways to get their kids engaged with activities that don't involve adding even more screen time into their children's lives.

This issue often seems to come up when talking with parents of kids who adore Minecraft. It's not only the game that they engage in, but also the YouTube videos and endless conversations that seem to start with the phrase, "Did you know in Minecraft. . . ." This is an especially challenging minefield to walk for adults, as many of us grew up playing PacMan, Nintendo, and other video games; adults love their smartphones and tablets as much as the kids do. Within the last year or so, there have been articles making the rounds on Facebook and other social media sites about parents who work for large tech firms being low-tech parents, many not allowing their children any computer/tech time at all (Bilton 2014).

An interesting counterpoint to this picture, though, is Minecraft. When Microsoft purchased Minecraft, their new CEO Satya Nadella remarked that Minecraft is "the one game that parents want their kids to play" (Soper 2014). He went on to make remarks about Minecraft being the best way to introduce STEM and to spark curiosity. This link to education is in the process of being made by Microsoft, as in 2015 they introduced Minecraft in Education. While there is little content available on the website at this time, it's clear they will be pursuing a path that is already being taken by some educators. The Microsoft Minecraft in Education portal can be found at http://education.minecraft.net.

While there has been a lot written about teachers using Minecraft in schools to teach a variety of subjects and engage students, public libraries have also been incorporating the game into their programming, especially those aimed at tweens and teens. Libraries are setting up servers, offering competitions, and time for kids and teens to come in and build together in the game. This is a great way to introduce the game to the library community and offer a service that will get kids in the often elusive demographic group of elementary school–age boys into the library. By having a library server, you can also put parents at ease by offering an opportunity for kids to play with other kids in a safe and moderated environment. You can offer many of the things that interest kids about multiplayer options, while limiting access to your world and being able to enforce rules to keep everyone safe and having a good time.

Minecraft Servers and Offering Gameplay in the Library

When we launched our Makerspace in 2013, hosting a server was something we were not ready for, and I did not feel we had the knowledge, staff, or volunteers to be able to run one in a meaningful way. As of this writing, we are preparing to launch a server in the library in the next year. Having become part of the Connected Camps Summer of Minecraft network, the library picked up some of the cost to give kids who participate in our Minecraft IRL Club access to the Connected Camp summer camp experience. Parents chose to either split the per-child cost to participate and others paid the entire cost of participation. As an educator partner, we received a discount to provide access to the program for our users. In order to keep our costs down, we only offered a limited number of split-the-cost seats and filled those up. This camp appealed to parents and grandparents, who had not yet allowed their kids to take the plunge and purchase Minecraft access at home. We gave the kids access to the game by setting up camp accounts with the Minecraft licenses we had purchased through MinecraftEDU. If you have your own server, Connected Camps also offer the option to run the program on your own. They offer resources to help you get started as well as support to help you have a successful program. Our goal is to be up and running with teen or adult volunteers to run the program on our own next year, as well as host challenges throughout the year to tie-in with our IRL club or other activities going on at the library or in the community.

Setting up a server, finding people to be moderators, and figuring out just how to offer gameplay can be a bit intimidating and may not be practical in all library settings. There are many questions to answer before rolling out a Minecraft server to your library users. Connected Camps Educator Program (http://connectedcamps.com/educators/) is a great place to start, if you are looking to set up a server and run an in-game Minecraft program at your library. You can choose to join their Educator Network, which includes a variety of benefits such as access to the complete facilitator guides and support from the staff and counselors. Even if you do not wish to join as an affiliated educator, the website has some great resources, including videos on setting up a server, running in-game challenges, and even on how to run a coding camp. There are a lot of librarians doing this and resources out there to get you started. If you are looking specifically for librarians who are using Minecraft in their programming, the Facebook group Minecraft in Libraries (https://www.facebook.com/groups/minecraftin libraries/) is a great place to get ideas and tips for running a Minecraft server in your library.

One of the big questions you need to answer is the most basic: "why?" Many libraries have boards that will balk at the idea of spending money and devoting resources to this type of activity in the library, and you need to have a good argument in place as to why this is a service your library should offer. Thinking about the answer to this question will lead you thinking about the logistics of the service.

- Who will set it up and maintain it?
- Will your server operate on a schedule?
- Will it be moderated?
- If so, how or by whom?

These are just some of the issues you need to consider in order to bring your Minecraft program to life.

For librarians looking to launch gameplay alongside real-life activities, a great place to start is Minecraft: Education Edition (http://education.minecraft.net). Minecraft: Education Edition is replacing MinecraftEDU the summer of 2016 and will become available to all educators later in the year. Minecraft: Education Edition will not only offer services that are aimed at teachers and school settings, but definitely has a place in libraries as well. Microsoft plans on offering this special version of Minecraft designed for use in classroom settings at $5 per user as of this writing. This special version of the game will be available for public and school librarians to purchase at this special price allowing you to purchase as many user seats as you need. The game will feature all the things kids love about Minecraft but have some special features that make it a great tool for educational settings. Some of the cool features listed on the Minecraft: Education Edition website include a special collection of blocks and enhanced multi-player where up to 30 players can collaborate and work together. Microsoft will also be offering tutorials for first-time Minecraft educators. If you are looking for ideas to get started with Minecraft: Education Edition, the resource page on the website includes some lesson plans to help get you started, including a lesson on Pixel Art and a Redstone Lodge. These two lessons tie-in nicely with IRL projects covered in this book.

For those of you who may be familiar with MinecraftEDU, this version of the game has been developed in collaboration with the Teacher Gaming people behind that version. As mentioned in the previous chapter, it's obvious that Minecraft is something that Microsoft CEO Satya Nadella believes in, and with the resources of Microsoft behind it, Minecraft: Education Edition has a bright future. One thing that Microsoft is not currently planning on offering with this version is the Hosting Service that was previously available with the EDU version.

21ST-CENTURY SKILLS IN THE LIBRARY

While running in game challenges and having a Minecraft server are one way of creating library programming around Minecraft, bringing in hands-on, real-life activities is another approach, which is a different approach to Minecraft programming that can help you introduce 21st century and other literacies to your programs. What are these 21st-century skills and how do they look in the library? According the Institute of Museum and Library Services (IMLS), there four broad sets of skills that can then be broken down into smaller, more specific pieces. IMLS breaks down the skills sets like this:

1. *Learning and Innovation Skills.* These are skills that tie into things like critical thinking, problem solving, creativity, and innovation as well as the ability to communicate and collaborate with others. They also add visual, scientific, numerical, and basic literacy as well as cross-disciplinary thinking. These are the kinds of skills that tie into being able to come up with creative solutions to problems using the knowledge you have leading to innovation and new ideas.
2. *Information, Media, and Technology Skills.* This area ties into the ability to assess and evaluate information as well as the ability to use and manage that information. Being able to not only analyze media messages, but also the ability to choose and use the correct media creation tools to relay information as well as the ability to apply technology in an effective way are the areas covered by these skills.
3. *21st-Century Themes.* Besides global awareness, you will find more literacies here, including those needed for financial and entrepreneurial success as well as civic, health, environmental, and basic literacy.
4. *Social and Cross-Cultural Skills.* These are more social skill areas that are important for one to have to work with a diverse group of people from different backgrounds. Important skills in this area

include flexibility and adaptability, initiative and self-direction, productivity, accountability, leadership, and responsibility. (Institute of Museum and Library Services 2014)

This is a lot to take in, and perhaps not all of these skills are priorities for your library. So, you may wish to adapt it to your own purposes, but it offers a good starting point.

The projects and ideas presented in this book demonstrate that Minecraft programming can help you introduce and work with many of these skills. The skills that come up over and over again do not include the ability to use computers or use cutting-edge technology, and are not even about having knowledge in a specific area such as STEM. Instead, the focus is on those skills that can only be developed through doing. Nearly every set of 21st-century skills agree that the following skills are the most important:

- Collaboration and Teamwork
- Creativity
- Critical Thinking
- Problem Solving

In order to be a successful 21st-century citizen, people need to be able to work collaboratively in a team, use their imaginations to think creatively and critically, and last be able to use all of these to solve problems. While these are the four most important skill areas, the others on the IMLS list do come into play. You can explore and develop many of these other skills through hands-on learning using Minecraft.

The library is perfectly poised to help develop these kinds of skills through programming. The skills also tie into the Maker Mindset previously discussed. Makers learn by doing through trial and error, problem solving, and creative thinking. By tying into not only the Maker Movement, but also to 21st-century skill building, libraries approach education through a different door than in a formal education setting. As overheard during a presentation at the World Maker Faire, you only need to be a step ahead of the kids in order to be successful. This is so true! By being just that one step ahead, you have enough knowledge to introduce an activity, but not too much knowledge that you are walking participants through an activity step-by-step. Not having all the answers at your fingertips can be a very liberating experience, and a great way to get the kids problem solving and searching out their own answers. It allows you to better guide them rather than taking over whatever it is they are doing.

Minecraft IRL and Learning and Innovation Skills

Minecraft IRL is a great way to hone those learning and innovation skills as outlined by IMLS. The programs can be presented in a number of ways, introduced first to develop some of the skills, and then reintroduced in a less structured way where the kids guide the learning. Once kids have got down the basics of how a circuit works, you can introduce a variety of activities and challenges that can be explored through collaboration, trial and error, and creativity.

These programs can also touch on a number of literacies in just one program. For instance, documentation of an activity is an important part of maker programs. Experiment with a video camera or even a digital camera and invite the kids to record anything they find interesting, exciting, and more. You can collect the videos and pictures they record and not only share it with your community, but also you can then bring these in for another program where the kids can work with their recordings to create something new, developing not only visual literacies skills, but also moving into the next set of skills, information, media, and technology.

Minecraft IRL and Information, Media, and Technology Skills

Media and technology skills are two of the most obvious tie-ins to Minecraft programming in the library. There are thousands of YouTube Minecraft videos, unofficial books, wikis, and more related to Minecraft. YouTube is changing the way our kids not only entertain themselves, but also is a major source of information for many of them. In a program where kids can work hands-on with creation tools to make their own YouTube videos, create stop–motion animations, or record their own podcast, you can fully explore and grow these skills. You can also explore the process and what it takes to bring even something as seemingly easy as a YouTube video to life, so that it is something that people want to watch. Later, we'll explore the connection between information, media, and technology skills through storytelling activities.

Minecraft IRL and 21st-Century Themes

Libraries spend a lot of time cultivating and honing 21st-century literacies through various programs. Minecraft can be used to bring these themes to life in a variety of ways. The very nature of maker programs and the way you set up your program space can encourage kids to learn how to work collaboratively and learn from one another. If you choose to set up a Minecraft server, you have even more opportunities to encourage and develop global awareness and even civic literacy, by having the kids establish rules to be followed by all players on the server and set up a challenge or activity that can help reinforce the ideas of community.

You can even do the same for your club, if you choose to run it this way. Put the kids in charge of establishing the rules, consequences for breaking the rules, as well as even establishing what it is that the kids would like the club to be about. Or consider running a Mini Minecon at the library. By giving the kids the opportunity to have a stake at what happens in the club or at the Mini Minecon, and creating a small world within the library where they can learn what it means to be a citizen—you lay the groundwork for civic literacy and even global awareness. Running a Minecon also cultivates entrepreneurial and business skills in participants, as they learn what it takes to put together a convention of sorts. The kids can decide whether they will charge an admission fee or will create small items to sell to attendees. Set a budget for the event and teach the kids how to work within that budget as they plan the activities that take place at their convention.

Health and Environmental literacy may seem like more a stretch, but the open-ended nature of Minecraft even provides openings for those areas. Minecraft worlds have a variety of biomes, including aquatic, desserts, forests, and grasslands. Why not tap into these to make a connection to real-world biomes? Rocks and minerals, gardens, animals—all are major players in the Minecraft world and can open the door to learning all kinds of things. Even health literacy can be brought in. For example, Steve needs to eat and he turns pigs into pork chops, or he can make a cake, eat watermelon, and more. Food programs are always a lot of fun and popular with youngsters. Use Minecraft as a springboard to learning skills need to prepare or grow your own food.

Minecraft IRL and Social and Cross-Cultural Skills

Social and cross-cultural skills are ones that your kids will be engaging with at many Minecraft-based programs. Through working in groups on a variety of projects and activities, children will have the chance to work on learning when to listen and speak, respecting others' ideas, and being respectful to one another. When patrons participate in a Makerspace program at the Middletown Free Library, they sign a release and participation form, which not only serves as a safety and photo/video release, but is also an agreement between the maker and the library. Every young maker not only agrees to be safe and respectful to their fellow makers, but they also agree to take some responsibility for keeping the space safe for everyone. They are not only held accountable for their own actions, but also to be sure that others are being safe and respectful. They are asked to nicely remind a fellow maker about the rules or to be safe if needed. They are learning responsibility and how to handle these issues on their own, to teach others how to behave, and be safe through example.

The best way to ensure that you will be able to really build these 21st-century skills rests not only on the topics and themes your programs cover, but also in the way you facilitate the programming. Fostering skills is not only done through the interactions with participants, but also depends on the way you set up the space for an activity. Design your programs and your space to encourage as much collaboration and exploration as possible. One of the ways you can do this is to place materials needed for the project in common areas giving the kids the opportunity to interact with one another and see what others are working on. Your role as a librarian in these programs is to be more of a guide than a teacher. In running your programs in this way, you will also be learning as you go, tweaking the way you do things as you go. One thing you may wish to do is to keep a program journal where you can record what went well, what did not, and what you would try the next time you do the program.

Moving from a more formal "teacher" or program director role to facilitator can be challenging. Work on your own observation skills, and learn how and when to step in to provide guidance. Learn how to ask the right questions to put the learner on a path where they can make their own discoveries and come up with their own solutions. Ask more questions to help guide the learner to the solution, rather than providing the answer. For example, in working with circuits, if participants don't get the desired result, rather than pointing out where they went wrong, guide them through the troubleshooting process by asking a question about their work, which can help them make the connection to what should happen and where their project went off track. Sometimes, all you need to do is clear extra materials from the workspace in order for kids to find solutions. Other times it may take several tries to get at the problem and make the correction.

In setting up your space for an activity, arrange things so collaboration and interaction between participants can take place. Rather than setting up separate tables with a set of supplies at each table, put the supplies on tables around the perimeter of the room, so participants need to move around the space to get what they need for their project. This leads to a natural kind of interaction between participants. By having to move around, they see what others are working on, which can lead to discussions about their projects, a new collaboration, or even provide answers to roadblocks in the creation process.

One of the most important things to keep in mind when running programs that will work on developing the main 21st-century skills is to go into the program with an outline of what you would like to accomplish, but *not* a lesson plan. Don't be afraid to step back and let things unfold, and travel in a direction other than the one you envisioned going into the program. Put the kids in the driver's seat and let their interests and passions guide the process. This can be scary at first, but it really works in the end. You may find yourself with a room of loud kids (it may seem chaotic at times), but these are some of the most popular programs and are often the ones where the most learning is going on. The kids are engaged and having fun while gaining valuable skills at the same time.

Minecraft is the perfect vehicle for bringing maker programs to your library. The love the kids have for anything involving Minecraft allows you the freedom to create programs that are either closely tied to the game or just loosely taking off from it. Minecraft is the hook that gets them in the door, and once you have them coming and engaging in this kind of programming, they will want to come back again and again.

REFERENCES

Bilton, Nick. 2014. "Steve Jobs Was a Low-Tech Parent." *New York Times.* September 10. Accessed August 2015. 10. http://www.nytimes.com/2014/09/11/fashion/steve-jobs-apple-was-a-low-tech-parent.html?_r=0.

Institute of Museum and Library Services. 2014. "Museums, Libraries and 21st Century Skills." *Institute of Museum and Library Services.* Accessed November 10, 2015. https://www.imls.gov/impact-imlsnational-initiatives/museums-libraries-and-21st-century-skills/museums-libraries-and-21st-century-skills-definitions.

Soper, Taylor. 2014. "Microsoft CEO Satya Nadella on Minecraft: 'It's the one game parents want their kids to play.'" *GeekWire.* September 15. Accessed August 22, 2015. http://www.geekwire.com/2014/microsoft-ceo-satya-nadella-minecraft-one-game-parents-want-kids-play/.

3

Minecraft and Learning
in an Informal Environment

Minecraft in Real Life (IRL) activities are well suited to an informal learning space such as the public library, the school library, or after school clubs. Public libraries are not tied to curriculums, and it does not matter if a project is completed since there is no grade at the end of a program. While I am less familiar with school libraries, they are often the place where Makerspaces and maker programs take root in the school setting. In an informal space, learners are free to explore a topic, make mistakes, and create the project as they see it since there are no requirements except having fun.

Since the role of the librarian running the program is to be a facilitator rather than a teacher, you do not need to be an expert with all the answers. The direction of the program is really led by the kids participating—they are the leaders and in control of where the program goes. In these programs, give the kids the space to learn through trial and error and simply guide the learning process. Let the kids work together to come up with solutions, find answers, and essentially be learners and teachers.

As American education, especially in the public school setting, continues to focus on testing as a means of holding teachers accountable and measuring success, our kids are left behind in areas they would most profit from. American education is stuck in preparing students to enter a knowledge economy that no longer exists. Innovative and creative companies are not necessarily concerned with what a prospective employee knows, but with what they will do with what they know. In Tony Wagner's book *Most Likely to Succeed*, he discusses that "smart creatives" (as coined by Eric Schmidt and Jonathan Rosenberg in *How*

Google Works) are the kinds of people most sought after by today's companies (Wagner and Dintersmith 2015). Wagner discusses the idea that, with the growth of the Internet and knowledge literally at our fingertips, knowledge in and of itself is no longer valued as it once was. People who can take the knowledge they have and use it to employ creative solutions to problems are the people who will be successful in this new economy. Unfortunately, those setting education policies have doubled down on the knowledge economy by focusing on testing rather than giving kids the opportunities to hone their abilities to solve problems creatively, learn through failure, and teamwork.

To plan a Minecraft IRL program, you needn't lay out a complete lesson plan as you would if you were preparing to teach a classroom full of students at a school. Approach the planning process by first formulating and idea of the topic you will cover or that you want to explore. For some programs, you might create a set of instructions for yourself, so you know what all the steps are from your point of view as the kids may encounter different challenges or even take a different approach in their process. For example, you might have a set of instructions to follow for a soft circuit or paper circuit project that lays out the steps of creating the project. However, while you may start your project by drawing or planning out your design, another person might start by formulating their idea in their head or figuring out how they want to lay the circuit rather than focusing on the overall design of the finished project. By going in with an outline rather than a formal plan, you can allow the program to move at the pace and in the direction the kids want to take it. If you are doing multi-part programs that rely more on the creative process than creating a project, this is especially helpful. For example, when working with storytelling programs, you really don't need to rely on any kind of plan. You can introduce a topic (e.g., "If you were to create a movie that takes place in Minecraft, what would it be about?"), and then let the kids form teams or work on their own to come up with their ideas. The kids will work together and come up with ideas on their own and work with the materials on hand. Sometimes, they may start out working in smaller groups, but end up creating the final project in a larger, newly formed group. When our club explored stop–motion movie making, the project was planned to take part over several club sessions. Due to the nature of the club in my library, we don't always have the same kids at each club session, so by the time they were ready to film, a new group formed and they worked together to create the movie. Each member of this new team played a part and they pulled in ideas that they had been working on over the course of the project, came up with new ideas, and created a new final project.

Focusing on the process rather than the project is a new idea for many people working in libraries. For years, librarians have run craft programs from the final project backward, trying to get the kids to all create the same craft rather than focusing on exploration of materials and ideas. While there is some value to a "kit" or more structured project to build skills, such as sewing skills in the Minecraft Light-Up Torch project, the idea is to have less structure and more room for exploration.

Like anything new, it can be uncomfortable to take this approach. While there has been a push to promote this way of working with preschool children, it is a newer approach to working with older kids. After you work with the idea of process rather than project, you will see it can be quite freeing. You present the challenge, provide the materials, and then see what happens. Not only does this give the participants ownership over their work, but also it allows them to develop those other, less tangible 21st-century skills that are just as important for today's kids and teens to develop.

Now, not all the projects discussed in this book are "process projects," but many can be approached that way or can be a combination of process and project. For instance, when working with e-textiles or circuit projects, there is a certain amount of teaching and more project-based elements to it. A circuit works in a certain way and there are rules which need to be followed if the end product is going to work, but even in these projects, there is plenty of room to focus on process more than project. The kids are exploring a new medium and your first project that introduces a new element may be more project based, where everyone is creating a specific item. However, once they have the basics down, you can reintroduce that topic in various ways, as the kids will have knowledge of how a circuit works and be able to focus more on the creative process rather than the technical process. Focusing on process also leaves room for the kids to make errors, troubleshoot, and figure out how something works. You will likely find that this kind of program is not only more engaging, but also more fun. It will look different and definitely be louder than a more traditional craft program. You may also find that it feels chaotic at times, but this is a sign that something wonderful is happening and your kids are learning.

For some educators and librarians, the idea of not coming into a program with a complete plan and all the answers can be a challenge.

It's important to keep in mind that as facilitator, you are to help guide the kids to the answers rather than providing the answer yourself. While you cannot go into a program with no knowledge, you only need to be a step ahead of the participants to be successful. You will learn a new approach to problem solving and learn how to ask questions that get kids thinking and looking for solutions. It is also beneficial to show kids that as adults we do not always know all the answers, but as a group we can try to discover answers together or even leave them with the challenge of finding an answer and presenting it the next time you meet.

DESIGNING PROGRAMS FOR LEARNING AND FUN

When setting up a program space to encourage collaboration and creativity, there are some basic things to think about. Just as you want to plan your programs to allow for creative thinking by leaving ideas and programs a bit open ended, you should also consider how to set up your program space in a manner that encourages collaboration and engagement. If all the materials are on each table and the kids are left to sit at a table for 60–90 minutes, you are placing limitations on sharing and collaboration. In this scenario, participants may work with the other kids at their table, but they do not get a chance to see what others are working on and get ideas or engage with those outside their area. Of course, we cannot go back and redesign our libraries' learning spaces for tinkering, but you can draw some ideas from places such as the Exploratorium's Tinkering Studio for ideas on how to set up your space for a learner-driven program. For example, one of the projects you might wish to explore incorporating Minecraft is paper circuits. The Tinkering Studio's blog post on working with paper circuits will explain how they set up this kind of program, why, and how it worked in their space (http://tinkering.exploratorium.edu/tinkering/2012/10/10/beyond-the-museum-tinkering-with-paper-circuits). One of the great things about their approach to space is that you can incorporate elements of their ideas into active as well as passive maker activities in your library, precisely because they moved their activities out of a controlled workshop and onto the museum floor itself.

The Exploratorium describes the learning in their space as a process that inspires inspiration, creativity, frustration, and breakthrough. This process is exactly what Minecraft IRL activities are based on, so their approach provides a good model for planning space and programs. Activities in the Tinkering Studio are based on learners' prior interest and knowledge. (Petrich, Wilkinson, and Bevan 2013). By basing library activities around Minecraft, you are using your participants' interest and knowledge of Minecraft in different ways, some of them unexpected, which encourage learning and exploration.

Another technique that the Exploratorium uses is to allow users to explore and create through multiple pathways. Participants can choose from a variety of materials or there are a variety of pathways or outcomes that allow for learners to direct the activity (Petrich, Wilkinson, and Bevan 2013). In Minecraft IRL programs, you can achieve this in a variety of ways, depending upon the activity being explored. This does not mean there are endless possibilities or no structure, but just that there are multiple ways to explore a project that encourage engagement and creativity. For example, you might provide stations where the kids can choose activities, allowing them to move around and discover an activity that interests them. You can also provide a variety of materials to use in completing the project or activity. For example, in a program on 3D Printing and Design, you might offer iPads and computers with different CAD programs or apps available, so that the kids can approach the process from different ways and find the program that they are comfortable working with to produce a finished design.

While you may not be able to change the color palette or physical design of your space, there are ways to set up your programming area that enhances learning through doing and helps build 21st-century skills. To get the wheels turning and ideas flowing, show some examples from the activity you will be working on or from similar activities. It's hard to work from a blank slate, so putting a piece of paper in front of someone or even sitting them in front of a program like Tinkercad can leave many feeling overwhelmed and with no idea where to start. We recently held a toy take apart program, where the kids were taking apart old toys and creating new toys from the old. Before we started, I showed some slides of creations others had made in a Makerspace to give them an idea of what is possible. In an informal learning situation, your goal is to guide and inspire, but you also want to avoid keeping things so wide open that kids give up because they do not have an idea of what to do or where to start.

Also, consider how you set up your tables and work area to invite collaboration and discussion (Petrich, Wilkinson, and Bevan 2013). You can actually set up your tables so that the kids will naturally work together. Rather than setting each seat up with a set of tools and materials, put all the materials that they may need in the center of the table. Every child does not need their own pair of scissors or tools, and if they have to talk with each other to obtain the tool they wish to work with or need, it helps to kick-start the collaboration process. Kids will ask each other about what they are creating, and will often end up combining projects and working together. They will learn to ask each other for help and become natural facilitators of the activity.

Another way to set up your space to encourage collaboration and exploration is to only place a few tools at the tables. Then, place craft materials or other supplies for the project at the front of the room. With this arrangement, kids have to get up and find what is available. They will walk by other tables and get a chance to see what others are working on. They may stop to ask questions and find out more about the other things being created. Having the materials in a central location gives them another opportunity to spark conversation. Placing materials at a central location also encourages autonomy because kids can revisit the supply table as many times as they want, checking out the various items available as their ideas develop or their thinking about the project changes. Putting all the materials around the edges of the space and in a common area allows for evolution of ideas, collaboration, problem solving, and more because you are encouraging discovery. When the supplies are just at their work table, participants are less likely to explore materials that are not on the table and may not even ask if other supplies are available.

One of the drawbacks to this approach can be the kid who hordes all the materials at his or her workspace. It can be tempting for some kids to gather all the supplies they think they may want to use for their project and then go off to the corner to work. This problem tends to arise in programs where you may have a limited supply of a certain material, for example, when working with littleBits, you may only have a few buzzers but many lights, and one child may scoop up all the buzzers that they may need even if they have not yet formulated a complete plan for their project. While it can be difficult to get some kids to give up the supplies they are not using, you will need to approach that participant and convince them to give up some of the coveted item. You would handle this kind of situation the same way you would in any program where this situation comes up. You can either approach the child when you see them take a large quantity of a limited supply by either having them give up some of the excess pieces or you can inform them that they can work with the materials for now, but will need to give up some pieces if another child wishes to use them. If you have limited supplies, it is sometimes best to put those at each table rather than leaving everything up for grab to prevent such a situation from arising in the first place.

Last, as discussed earlier, how you facilitate your program is key to encouraging learning in an informal environment. This is probably the hardest part of running informal learning activities, as it differs from the librarian's usual way of conducting programs, and it takes some time to get used to. To become a good facilitator, spend some time observing the way the kids work in your space or how they are approaching a particular project. This can give you an idea of what they know already and will help you guide them in the right direction. Being a facilitator does not mean you cannot show someone how to do something, but rather than completing the task for them, you might show them a couple of ways to work with a material and then give them room to get started. You have probably seen activities where adults are working with kids the unfortunate outcome when the child asks for help and the adult ends up taking over the project or activity. While this may get the task completed more quickly or neatly, this is not what good facilitation looks like. If you have adults volunteering or parents staying to help in your space, be sure to familiarize them with how facilitation looks. It may be natural to want to jump in and help when you see someone getting frustrated, but it's vital to not jump in too quickly. Frustration is part of the process when you are running a program where you want kids to learn through trial and error. Often, our biggest breakthroughs in learning happen when we make mistakes and work to find the solution.

Process learning often means going back to the drawing board several times, experimenting with different tools or materials, until getting the end product one wants. If you are worried that kids are not learning anything, regroup with them at the end of the program to reflect on the day's activity. This reflection can offer insight into what the kids found meaningful, what they enjoyed, and even what frustrated them in working with the activity. The Tinkering Studio has identified four indicators to look at when evaluating programs for success. These are:

- Engagement, including expressions of joy, wonder, frustration, and curiosity
- Intentionality, which is the variation of efforts, personalization of the project, and evidence of self-direction
- Innovation—Do you see the kids repurposing tools or ideas, redirecting their efforts, and as time goes on are their projects or approaches more complex?
- Solidarity—Are they collaborating, sharing, and helping each other complete the project? (Petrich, Wilkinson, and Bevan 2013)

These four ideas are a great place to start when planning your programs and measuring success. By talking to the kids and their parents as well as through observation, you can get an idea of how well things are going. By reflecting and evaluating as you go along, you will be able to put what you learn into improving your programs and your own facilitation skills.

By employing the methods of process learning through designing programs that are fun, encourage creativity, and let the kids take the lead, you will go a long way to not only having a great program, but also give your patrons a place where learning can take place in a way it cannot in a more formal setting. It's going to be noisy and it may seem disorganized, but these are really the signs of a great program. The noise and chaos are indications of engagement with the activity and a sure sign you are doing something right!

REFERENCES

Petrich, Mike, Karen Wilkinson, and Bronwyn Bevan. 2013. "It Looks Like Fun, But Are They Learning?" In *Design, Make, Play: Growing the Next Generation of STEM Innovators*, ed. Margaret Honey and David E. Kanter, 238. New York: Routledge.

Wagner, Tony, and Ted Dintersmith. 2015. *Most Likely to Succeed: Preparing Our Kids for the Innovation Era.* New York: Scribner.

4

Minecraft, 3D Printing, and 3D Design

3D printing is a fascinating and quickly evolving area of technology. The 3D Printer is the one device that most people associate with Makerspaces. Today, the market has exploded and there are printers to fit almost every budget. So, if you are interested in purchasing a 3D Printer for your library, there are now more options than ever. *MAKE:* magazine does an annual "3D Printer Shootout" every Fall to see which printers are the best, testing for a variety of factors, including print quality, ease of use, and price. 3D Printers can now be purchased through Amazon, Staples, and even at your local Home Depot. You can add a 3D Printer to your library for under $1,000, with the upkeep and ongoing costs minimal. It's a technology that is here to stay and is becoming more and more mainstream.

A 3D Printer is a great tool to introduce to your library community. It acts as a hook to attract attention and people to your programs and even into your library. Many people have heard the news stories about 3D Printing, but have not ever seen one. If you keep your printer out on the library floor and run print jobs, you will likely find people stopping to take a look and ask a lot of questions. This gives you a great opportunity for plugging various services and programs your library may offer. Having a 3D Printer available for public use can also be a great way to make connections with your local schools and homeschooling communities. Invite teachers to use it to create manipulatives for their classrooms or ask them to refer students to the library to use it to create projects. The homeschooling community, in particular, is interested in anything that can help them with science and technology subjects, so you may find people coming to your library to check it out that you may not have seen before.

While there are many benefits to having a 3D Printer as part of your library's technology offerings, there are some issues to consider before taking the plunge. 3D printing, like any technology, requires someone on your staff who will take time to learn how to use the printer and troubleshoot problems. Printer companies vary as to the quality and amount of support they offer to customers, so you may find yourself on your own in figuring out why the printer is not extruding or dealing with various other issues that come up. A company may offer great support, but when you run into trouble, they will most likely be shipping you a part with instructions for making the repair yourself. Try to overcome your fear of breaking the machine, and dive in and figure out the problem.

Another consideration before making a purchase is how many printers are right for your space. If you have not used a 3D Printer before, be aware that the time it takes for an item to print out is longer than you might think. With limited program time, it can be challenging to print everyone's creations and have them walk out with a finished object, unless you have multiple printers or are printing something small.

Last, consider the future of 3D printing in your library. There are expenses beyond the initial purchase price—for example, costs involved with filament replacement and the possible expenses if something goes wrong and you need to contact support or make a repair. Some companies offer extended protection plans, but weigh the costs versus the benefits of such a plan. You should have an idea of reliability after having the printer running for a period of time which will help you make that decision. The other "expense" is staff time and responsibilities. Who will be offering programs or demonstrations, who is responsible for maintaining the equipment, and so forth.

So, what if you haven't jumped on the 3D Printer bandwagon? The great news is that you can still introduce 3D design to your club in various ways. At the end of the day, learning the design process is really the most important part of the process. Kids who are playing Minecraft are already familiar with 3D design because, despite what people think when they see the graphics, Minecraft is a 3D world. While they are limited in the shapes they can use in building, they are already thinking in 3D when they build in the game. You can use this as a springboard to introduce 3D design to your club even if you don't have a 3D Printer. There are a wealth of videos online that introduce 3D Printers and show how a printer works that allow you to show the end part of process without having a printer on site. Here are a few good examples:

- Future Engineers Challenge 3D Printing Page—http://www.futureengineers.org/Learn/Printing
- Funk-e Studios "What is 3D Printing and how does it work?"—https://youtu.be/Llgko_GpXbI
- Shapeways, "How 3D Printing Works"—https://youtu.be/BTTnaI4EYnY

There are also printing services that you can send designs to for printing such as Shapeways (http://www.shapeways.com), Ponoko (3D prints and laser cutting; http://www.ponoko.com), and i.materialise (http://i.materialise.com), or you can search the web to see if there is a site nearby that allows the public access to their printers, perhaps setting up an off-site meeting. Most prosumer model printers are pretty portable, so it would even be worth inquiring whether a local Makerspace or college could bring a printer to your location for your club to see.

WHAT IS 3D PRINTING?

3D printing is sometimes known as "additive manufacturing." It is called additive because unlike other manufacturing methods where you are using a tool, such as a laser cutter to take material away, a 3D Printer starts with a flat surface and an object is built by the machine by adding layers of materials to the surface. Most 3D Printers you find in public libraries print in plastic. The printer takes the plastic filament through an extruder which is heated to about 230 degrees Celsius. The extruder melts the plastic and then adds it in layers to the print plate to create your object. The most common type of plastic used in these printers is PLA, which is short for polylactic acid. This is plastic that is plant based—made from plants such as corn, potatoes, wheat, or other starchy grains. If you are concerned about the ecological implications of 3D printing and plastic, it's best to use a printer that can print in PLA. Unlike some other types of plastics used in 3D printing, such as ABS (acrylonitrile butadiene styrene), PLA is not petroleum based. There are other advantages to PLA:

- It releases fewer greenhouse gases and takes less energy to produce than plastic soda bottles.

- PLA plastic may be recyclable and is biodegradable in commercial compost.
- It is considered nontoxic.
- It is safe for printing indoors.

As you can see from this list, PLA is a great choice for 3D printing in library Makerspaces.

However, there are some reasons why you may wish to print using ABS. It's a stronger and more flexible plastic. ABS is the same kind of plastic that LEGOs are currently made out of; however, it's interesting to note that LEGO is currently looking to phase out ABS, replacing it with a more sustainable and environmentally friendly plastic (Dockrill 2015). If you need a strong plastic with a higher melting point, ABS can be useful, but do consider the downsides that make it less ideal for use in libraries. Printers that can print in ABS are often enclosed on all sides. This is because the extruder(s) and the print bed must be heated in order to get a good print and the enclosure helps maintain the temperature. The downside to this is that there is a potential for injury if one is not careful, as it takes time for the finished object and the print bed to get cool enough to handle. There have also been concerns raised about possible negative health effects caused by breathing in ultrafine particles that are released into the air when printing with ABS. While you don't want to use any 3D Printer in an enclosed space, this is especially important if printing with ABS. Besides the possible dangers posed by ultrafine particles, the plastic has a strong odor to it, which may be bothersome to some people. While there are no definitive studies proving that ABS printing is dangerous to one's health, it's best to consider that there are concerns. If you are using ABS in your library, carefully consider the ventilation available and consider purchasing or creating an enclosure for the printer. There are some kinds of print jobs that are more suited to printing in ABS, as it's a stronger and more flexible plastic than PLA, but for use in the library, PLA is really the way to go—it is environmentally friendly, smells pleasant when printing, and there is little to worry about in way of adverse health effects.

Once you have access to a printer, you need something to print. You can design something yourself in one of many different CAD (computer-aided design) programs, or you can use various apps that allow you to design and print, or you can visit a site such as Thingiverse, where people share their design files for others to print and sometimes they even allow other users to modify their designs. There are special file types used by CAD software that most printer manufacturers allow you to print from. In order to print an object, you must prepare your file such that your printer can read it. Most printers can print designs that originate as an. STL or. OBJ file. STL or STereo-Lithography is a triangulated representation of a 3D CAD file. This is the most common file type used in 3D printing. Most printer software also accepts files in the OBJ (or object file) format. OBJ files are often used in 3D graphics programs and are a data format that represents 3D geometrical shapes. Once you have your STL or OBJ file, you need to use software to prepare your file for printing and convert it to a file type that your printer can read. Many printers come with software that allows you to scale your finished object, add supports, and arrange your object on the print bed for optimal printing. Ideally, this software will offer a preview of some sort that estimates printing time, so you know how long a model will take to print out before sending it to the printer. Once your file looks the way you would like it to be, you are ready to send it to the printer.

The preceding instructions give you a very basic overview of the 3D printing process. We'll look a little more in-depth into preparing files for printing and design later in this chapter. Now that you have some background, you are ready to dive into the design process. There are many different options for 3D printing related to Minecraft. There are a number of ways to create objects in Minecraft for printing, or you can introduce your club to CAD programs to create their own designs. There are also apps on the computer and iPads that allow you to build or create items for 3D printing and more. If you don't have a 3D Printer, don't worry! You can always inform your club members and their parents about commercial printing service such Shapeways or iMaterialise. These companies will print your items for a fee and offer a wide range of material types for printing, everything from resin to plastics to metals. The costs can vary depending upon the materials you choose for printing, but as an example, a 1.25cm × 2.75 full color Creeper printed in resin would cost $5.73, plus about $5 in shipping to have printed by Shapeways. If 3D printing at the library is not a practical option for your community, there are ways to incorporate 3D design into your program that don't require a printer at all.

3D PRINTING FROM MINECRAFT

One way you can introduce 3D printing to your club is by building in Minecraft, and then exporting your designs to a printer or printing service. Kids using Minecraft are always busy creating cities, buildings,

8-bit art, and more. They would love to find a way to bring these creations to life outside the game, but probably don't know how to do that. Luckily, there are a couple of options for creating designs in Minecraft, and then printing them on a 3D Printer.

Printcraft

Printcraft is one of the options available to libraries that want to bring the game into the real world via 3D printing. Printcraft is a multiplayer server where players can build something, and then either receive their file for printing or send it to a print service for printing. When players join the server, they will see building plots marked out in the ground with glowstone. They will also see control panels at each of these plots. Players can claim a plot, build a creation, and then go to the control panel to print their creation. They can claim a plot so that other players cannot grief their creation; this means that they will have time to build before printing. Once they are finished and they have their STL files, they can clear and unclaim their plot, allowing others to build. If a player has claimed a plot, he or she can add a friend, so they can build together.

If you are planning to set up a server for your library and you are interested in incorporating 3D printing in your programming, Printcraft provides you with the files you need to add 3D printing capabilities to your Minecraft server, assuming you are already running one. They also provide a completely configured server for you to use. In order to add the files to your current server, you need to be running a type of server called craftbukkit. You would then download the plug-in and add it to your server. By adding the plug-in, you are adding the commands that allow you to print. Print a selection and load your model to the Printcraft server to display and print it. The completely configured server provided by Printcraft is based on one they are already using in their own workshops and with schools. It works well for small groups, such as the groups you would have in a library program. The world is smaller than the server that Printcraft runs, making it easier to manage in a small group setting. You can find the files to download at http://www.printcraft.org/resources.

Mineways

If you don't want to build new things for printing, but have Minecrafters who want to print things they've already built or you already have your own server that you kids are working on, then Mineways is the way to go. Mineways is an open-source program, and you will need to download to your computer in order to use it. Luckily, it is available in Mac, Linux, and PC versions, and it is free. Unlike Printcraft, you are not printing by using command blocks in Minecraft, rather you are mapping an area and then exporting that area for printing. One of the nice things about Mineways is that you can print from any of the Minecraft worlds you have already created. Use the Mineways tools to zoom in on the area you wish to print, then select it with the tool, and export it to be printed either by your own 3D printer or you can send it to Shapeways for full color printing. One of the other great things about Mineways is the extensive documentation and support available via the Mineways website. The creator has many YouTube tutorials, as well as written documentation available to help you get started and troubleshoot any issues you might run into—from downloading to fixing a design for printing. Another thing that you may find useful if you are going to use Minecraft for 3D printing in the library is the link to the workshop slides that Mineways uses in workshops with kids and adults using the program. These slides not only work in a Minecraft and 3D printing workshops, but also give you great tools to use when explaining Minecraft and 3D printing to your library board or director. They can be used to make the case for why both are great additions to the library, as well as to explain what they are and how they are related.

Mineways is a bit more complicated to use than Printcraft, but is fairly easy once you have it installed. If you are running antivirus software on your computer, such as Norton, you may need to change some settings in the firewall or download scanning in order to extract and install the file. This is because Mineways is an open-source software, which is read as a potential threat by some security software. In order to help you in creating a good file for 3D printing, you may wish to install a viewer that will help you see what you are doing, and figure out the exact settings you want for your 3D print file. The Mineways website suggests MeshLab as a good viewer for working with files that you extract from Minecraft using the Mineways software (http://meshlab.sourceforge.net/). MeshLab is an open-source software program used for processing and editing 3D mesh files. This software is often used with 3D scans, and includes tools for editing, cleaning, and working with your scans or unstructured files. When viewing your world in Mineways, it is very pixelated and it's difficult to see exactly what you are printing. When you open the file in MeshLab or another viewer, you can see a full color rendering of exactly what you extracted from your Minecraft world. If you are happy with the file, you are ready to send it to your 3D printer's software to prepare for printing. In your printer's software, you can adjust the scale of your design for the size you wish your creation to be. You may need to add supports in MeshLab or another viewer if your 3D printer's software doesn't have a way to add supports, and be sure your design has added these supports before sending the file to the printer. Once you have your completed print, you can use it with other library programs or send it home with your club member. If you are printing in one color, you can extend your program by having the club members print their designs in white and then have them add color to their creations using paint or permanent markers. If you send your design to a printing service, you can have them printed in resin in full color, such as the Eiffel Tower example on the Mineways website (http://bit.ly/mwsample).

3D Printing Apps for the Computer and Mobile Devices

If you are not ready to jump into designing using CAD software or web-based applications, you can always explore 3D design using a variety of apps that are not specifically Minecraft related, but are fun to explore. If you take a look at the workshop slides provided by Mineways (http://bit.ly/mwslides), you can see how to make a Minecraft-related learning jump by talking about additive versus subtractive manufacturing with the kids and have them give examples of each type related to a Minecraft building activity.

Cookie Caster

http://www.cookiecaster.com

You may have seen the Minecraft cookie cutters available through some online retailers and some booksellers. Cookie Caster is an easy way to get the kids creating and printing their own cookie cutters. There are two ways to create a cookie cutter using this app. You can use the pen tool to connect straight lines to create your shape. Once your lines are connected, you can add curves if you wish. The other way to create a custom cookie cutter is to either upload a JPEG and use the magic trace feature, or use the search feature to look for an image through the app. If you have an account with Thingiverse, you can then upload your design directly from Cookie Caster into your account for printing and sharing. Please note that it's not recommended to cut food directly with personal 3D printed items, as they have not been officially certified as food safe. It is recommended on the Cookie Caster site to either cover the dough with plastic wrap or the cookie cutter edges with aluminum foil.

Once you have created and printed the cookie cutters, you can use them in another Minecraft IRL program. If you are lucky enough to have access to a kitchen for use in programs or have a toaster oven, you can expand this activity to include cookie making. Making and rolling cookie dough is a great activity for kids. Add a STEM emphasis to the activity by talking about things, like the importance of accuracy in measurements and the science of baking itself.

If you don't have access to an oven or toaster oven for baking, you might go in a more artsy direction by using the cookie cutters as a mold to create window clings. To create the paint needed for this activity, all you need to do is mix a few drops of food coloring into your basic white school glue and mix, keep adding the food coloring and mixing until you get the desired color. The next step is to lay down some wax paper and have the kids fill the cookie cutters with enough paint to create a layer in the bottom of the cookie cutter. Let the shapes dry in the cookie cutters and once they are dry you will have your window clings, which the kids either bring home or decorate the libraries windows with.

Another non-cooking-related activity would be to create dough ornaments or decorations using the cookie cutters created with Cookie Caster. Like the baking activity above, you can have kids make the dough, focusing on measuring and mixing to get the right consistency. Since many dough recipes create white dough, you can add food coloring to the mixture to create colored dough. You could also just leave the dough white and the kids can paint or color their creations once they have dried. There are many recipes for dough ornaments that can be air dried, making clay cutouts an easy and inexpensive add-on activity. Here are a few easy and inexpensive dough recipes:

- White Clay Dough Ornaments on Happy Hooligans—http://happy hooligans.ca/white-clay-dough-ornaments/
- Clay-It-Now Baked and No Baked Salt Dough—http://www.clay-it-now.com/saltdoughrecipe.html
- Growing a Jeweled Rose No Cook Cinnamon Ornaments—http://www.growingajeweledrose.com/2013/11/no-cook-cinnamon-ornaments.html

Cube Team

If your library does not have any Minecraft accounts, and obtaining
Minecraft accounts is something that is not in your budget, Cube Team
is the next best thing. This app is also a great option if you don't have
the knowledge or ability to set up a Printcraft server. Cube Team is a
web-based app that allows players to create 3D paintings and models in a multiplayer environment. Unlike Minecraft, it's free, runs in
a web browser, and has a host of great editing tools allowing you
to build in an imaginative and massive environment. There are no
map constraints in Cube Team, and you can download OBJ files to
use with your 3D Printer. Another nice feature of this app is that you
can import images, 2D photos or 3D models, into the program, which
then will convert them into cubes. This cloud-based app works with
WebGL-based browsers, such as Firefox or Chrome, so be sure you are
using the most up-to-date version of your preferred browser before
you get started. Like Mineways, Cube Team's website includes great
documentation and support, including video tutorials that walk you
through every step of using the app.

   If you don't have a 3D Printer, but want to explore Cube Team, you
can also export your files and work on them in another program. Perhaps, you want to focus on editing or learning another type of design
software. Your club can export their Cube Team file as an OBJ file or
animated GIF. Like Printcraft and Mineways, you can print your creations on your own 3D printer or send them to a printing service to be
printed for a fee.

Blokify

If your library does not have a lot of computers or you are looking to
explore a variety of 3D design tools, consider this fun app available for
iPads from Cubify (http://blokify.com/). Unfortunately, this app is
not available for Windows or Android tablets at this time. It is a simple
app that allows you to create designs using blocks. The cube-shaped
blocks are the only shape available, but to add interest, you are building on a grassy platform and the blocks have features to make them
look like stones, wooden planks, and other features. This is another
fun and familiar way to introduce the kids into your club to designing
for 3D printing. If you don't have a lot of computers but have iPads
available, you can have some kids designing on the computers and
others on the iPads, and then they can switch off after a period of time.
One of the downsides of this app is that you are limited to the starter

play pack called Castle Mountain until you collect enough diamonds to unlock other play packs, or you can purchase more diamonds to unlock the other packs. Other play packs include Space Platform, Pirate Sea, and New Block City. You can print your designs by either sending them to a print service or by having the. stl file emailed to you or the design creator. You can also share your designs directly from the app to Facebook.

Tinkerplay

Available for Android, iPads, and Windows tablets.

Tinkerplay (http://www.123dapp.com/tinkerplay), a mobile app from Autodesk, lets kids easily design and create their own action figures. The parts are easily printed with no need for supports or raft materials, and it's easy to export your designs for easy printing with a number of printers. The app is designed to get kids creating right away by working with templates and modular parts to create their character. Once a child is comfortable with the app, or if they have more skills, they can create their own models rather than working solely with the professionally designed templates. One of the nice things about this app is that you can use it on mobile devices as well as in desktop environments. You can find the app in the Google Play, Apple's App Store, and in the Windows store. Like Blokify, this is a nice app to have available during 3D printing programs for kids to play with while waiting for their items to print. You might find some kids gravitate toward this kind of app than the more complicated design software. That's perfectly fine. This gives some new experiences with 3D design and can be a nice stepping stone for those not quite ready to dive into CAD software.

Tinkercad and Other Autodesk 123D Apps

Autodesk offers a suite of free 3D design tools for a variety of projects. You can use 123D Apps to design your own circuits, convert photos to 3D designs as well as designing your own objects for 3D printing. The 123D Apps include:

- 123D Design—a 3D creation and design tool for creating and customizing designs for 3D printing available for download on PC or Mac and as an iOS app
- 123D Make—turns 3D designs into 2D building plans for use with a laser cutter

- 123D Sculpt+—this is a 3D design tool for the iPad or Android mobile devices which lets you sculpt designs
- 123D Catch—this app is available as a PC download as well as for Apple, Android, and Windows mobile devices which lets you turn photos into 3D models
- 123D Circuits—web-based tool for learning electronics, especially good for learning Arduino and for use with Circuit Scribe conductive ink pen
- Tinkercad—similar to 123D Design, but perfect for beginners, this web-based app lets you create and customize designs for 3D printing and importing to Minecraft
- Meshmixer—downloadable software for Windows and Mac that lets you combine two or more 3D models to create new mashups as well as adding supports and getting your designs ready for printing

The Autodesk suite of free apps for 3D design and electronics makes it easy for you to introduce your club to the most exciting aspect of having a 3D Printer in the library—designing!! Printing out premade designs is a great way to introduce the process, but what you are really aiming for is getting their feet wet with the design process rather than just reproducing items that have already been designed. For the Minecraft in Real Life Club, you have an easy connection to Minecraft through the Tinkercad app. This app not only allows you to design for 3D printing, but also if you don't have a printer, your club members can download their design and then import it into their own or the library's Minecraft world.

Getting into the design process may seem intimidating if you have no background in using CAD programs, but rest assured, anyone can get the kids up and running with Tinkercad very easily. The first series of Minecraft IRL programs we launched introduced the kids to 3D printing and design with Tinkercad, and I have absolutely no background in engineering, design, or working with CAD programming. I would not call myself an expert by any means, but I jumped in and let the kids lead the way. Their experience building in Minecraft makes it easy for many of them to leap right in and experiment with the program. The only knowledge you really need to get started is being familiar with the basics of the program. Remember, part of what you are doing with this kind of programming is letting the kids learn through doing, trial and error, and collaboration, all of which they can do in learning a program like this.

If you are still uncertain and want to have some designs under your belt first, Tinkercad makes it easy to get started by offering tutorials as soon as your account is created. Also, check out Project Ignite, which was designed with educators in mind, a free platform to teach and build skills in young learners. There are step-by-step instructions for a variety of projects that will help you not only learn how to use Tinkercad, but also become familiar and comfortable with the tools available. Project Ignite gives you the tools you need to teach a project, including tips for how to best implement the project when teaching it to a group. You can set up a classroom and save projects to it, as well as invite club members to join your classroom to keep track of everyone's progress. I highly recommend starting with the button project for learning Tinkercad yourself. It's easy and buttons are familiar items, which helps the novice designer to stay on track and not get discouraged. If you are looking for a club project via the Ignite website, check out the Minecraft Bobblehead project, which is available to add to your classroom. And, if you are still looking for opportunities to learn more about Tinkercad, consider the Autodesk Tinkercad channel on YouTube featuring tutorials and tips. Finally, if your library has a Lynda.com subscription, you may wish to check out the class called "Up and Running with Tinkercad."

3D PRINTING MINECRAFT IN REAL LIFE PROGRAM

Day One of Program

Now that you are familiar with some of the tools available to introduce 3D design and printing to your space, you are ready for your first 3D printing program with your club. You can run this program without a printer and you'll find tips for alternate routes to take if you do not have a printer in your space.

Materials

- Book—*Leo the Maker Prince* by Carla Diana
- Computer and projector or monitor/TV
- Enough computers with a WebGL-enabled browser and Internet connections for your club (kids can work 2–3 to a computer)
- 3D printer (if you have one)
- Minecraft accounts (if working with Minecraft instead of the printer)

Begin the program by asking the kids if they know anything about 3D printing or if they have used or seen one before. Give the kids time to come up with some things they may have seen in the news, read, or heard about 3D printing. After this initial discussion, introduce them to 3D printing via the story of *Leo the Maker Prince*. You don't have to read the whole story as it's a bit long, but it gives a great introduction to 3D printing through a fun story, and then goes through various ways people are using the 3D printing in their homes and businesses.

After reading the story, note the Minecraft connection. You can do this by showing a YouTube video of 3D Printer created by the user ItsJustJumby in Minecraft using Redstone (https://youtu.be/NosYiy NXhzQ). You can also bring in discussion about how they are already designing in 3D when creating things in Minecraft.

The next step is to introduce the kids to the 3D Printer you have in your library space. Walk them through the basics, showing them the filament attached to the back where it goes into the extruder, how the extruder heats up the filament, and then builds the object on the platform. If it's a small group, you can give more detailed instruction, but it's best to keep it simple for larger groups and walk them through again when they are ready to print. Be sure to have a print job ready to go, so you can start a print while you are walking them through. There is always a lot of excitement for that first print!

> *If you don't have a printer*, *show some short videos of objects being printed on a 3D Printer and then move into the Tinkercad portion of the program, perhaps talking about printing services, if it's appropriate for your community.*

For the first 3D printing club meeting, I then introduce the kids to Thingiverse so they can get an idea of all the design possibilities. This also allows the kids to download a design to the computer, and then learn how to prepare it for printing using the 3D Printer's software. Search "Minecraft" on Thingiverse and then click on a design to show them how to download designs. Point out things they should pay attention to when looking at design pages in Thingiverse, such as reading the "Thing Details," "Instructions," and even the "Comments" sections, for hints and tips on creating the best print. You can also point out the "Remix It" tool that allows them to take a file and make changes to create a new thing, and of course the "Download" tab. Some of the files in Thingiverse are for laser cutters, so be sure to let the kids know that they will need to download an STL or OBJ file in order to print the item. Have the kids search for something they wish to print on Thingiverse and ask them to download it to their computer.

If you are going to have the kids print the items, you might wish to guide them toward choosing smaller items or things that can be scaled small so that everyone can walk away with a printed item. This would also be a good opportunity to show them any kind of Print Preview option, which can tell them approximately how long it will take to print out an item. You can then introduce the scaling tool, so they can shrink the item to a manageable size that fits the time frame you have available in your program. I would suggest limiting the kids to print jobs that take 10 minutes or less. Another way to do this is to choose something beforehand and have the file on all the computers so that the kids can get the experience with the 3D Printer software and you can get everyone a printed item.

Once the kids have downloaded a file, you are ready to introduce them to the 3D Printer software. Explain that 3D Printers all speak their own "language" and can't understand an STL or OBJ file, so the software translates the file into a language the printer can understand. Introduce them to the tools available in your printer's software, so they can see how the object can be further manipulated for printing, including duplicating an item on the bed so more than one object at a time can be printed. One of the most important tools you will want them to be familiar with is the scaling tool, since objects are often too large or too small for a good print. The biggest problem in the library is with objects that are too large and take too long to print. This step offers you a good opportunity to explain that 3D printing is not as quick as printing out a paper for a report and that they should keep this in mind when they are designing their own projects.

The other important things to keep in mind when you get to the printing stage are rafts and supports. These are two tools available in most 3D Printer software that will help you get better prints. The raft is a layer added to the bottom of a model that can help the object stick to the build plate and can help prevent warping that may occur as the object layers cool during the printing process. The raft is easily removed once the job is complete. Not all print jobs need rafts and they are best used when the object you are printing has a small base. Supports are important when you are printing something that has pieces that "hang" in the air. For instance, when printing a Minecraft pig, the head and belly are in the air with nothing underneath for the printer to build on. You cannot just add layers in the air, so a support is like a small column that is built from the base up to provide a base layer for those "hanging" pieces to be built on. If your 3D Printer's software does not provide an option for adding supports, you will need to use a program like Meshmixer (http://www.123dapp.com/mesh mixer) to add the supports before printing. For example, the Dremel Idea Builder software does not have a feature that adds supports for you, but if you try to send an object to the printer that may need supports, a dialog box will pop up referring you to Meshmixer to add supports to your model. Once they have downloaded and readied a print for printing, they are ready to start designing and printing their own designs and projects.

If you don't have a printer, rather than going through the how-to print lesson, why not issue a building challenge to your club? Once the kids have seen the videos of a 3D Printer in action, as well as the Redstone 3D printer in Minecraft, you can set them loose to see if they can come up with their own printer in the game. This gives you a great opportunity for a collaborative challenge. Have the kids work in teams on this one, and see what they come up with.

Day 2 of Introduction to 3D Design/Printing

At the second club meeting, you will really get into the design process. When we first started the club, we did not have as many computers available as I would like, so we definitely had to split the kids into pairs to work on their designs. We supplemented the lack of computers with four iPads that had Blokify installed on them. There are even more options for designing available now, so having a mix of iPads/ tablets and computers is a great way to go. There are several ways to implement the mix of tablets and computers. You can split the group up and have half working on the computers and half working with the tablets, and after a set amount of time have the kids switch. Or you can offer up both options and see what the kids gravitate toward, and let them figure it out on their own. You will likely have some kids that prefer working with one or two other people, and then there are those who want to work on their own. It's good to have some flexibility when it comes to this. You want the kids to be comfortable, have fun, and learn in the way that works best for them.

A full tutorial for using Tinkercad could be a book in itself, so rather than try to explain in detail, I will simply share some tips for getting started and things to keep in mind when working with the program. In order to use Tinkercad, you need to set up an account. You can sign on about three times to one account without running into problems. Either have the kids create their own accounts or have several library accounts set up so everyone can work on the program. Once you log in, you will be able to start a new project by clicking on "Create a new design." Click on that button and you are ready to get started with your creations.

You are now in the workplane, which will be a new way of designing for most of your kids. Building in Tinkercad is a bit different than building in Minecraft, so be sure to show them how to view their objects from all sides. When you are placing objects on top of one another, they may appear aligned or touching from one viewpoint, but when you rotate the workplane, you may see that they are not touching at all. Be sure the kids are aware that they will need to view their objects from all angles to make certain that everything is lined up. On the left hand side of the screen, you will see a round navigation button with arrows and a picture of a home. This button allows you to view your project from various angles. On the right hand side of the screen, a list gives you access to various shapes available for creating your designs. If you click on "Geometric," you will see a variety of geometric shapes available for building. Simply click on the one you want and drag it onto the workplane. Be sure to point out the "Group" and "Ungroup" buttons at the top of the screen, as these are very important to keep in mind when designing. When joining objects together, group them together so they become one instead of two separate pieces. An instance where you would want to group together the shapes is when you want to join individual parts to be one. This will keep the object together, so you don't accidentally take your creation apart and have to start over.

One last feature that bears noting is the "Edit Grid" feature at the bottom of the right hand side of the screen next to your workplane. If you are working with a particular printer, such as the Makerbot Replicator, you can set the grid to be the same as the size of your build plate on your printer under "Use a Preset." You can also customize it to the size for your particular printer. This helps ensure that the kids don't build something that won't fit the build plane of the printer you are using. You can also have the grid set at a smaller size, if you want to keep the designs small for faster printing, but that is always something you can scale once they are finished with their designs.

Once the kids have finished their designs, you are ready for 3D printing. To download the object, click on "Design" and a dialog box appears, which provides choices for the file format you wish to use.

There are four choices, but you will want to choose either .STL or .OBJ so you can import the design into your 3D Printer software. Other options in the Design menu include downloading for Minecraft as well as ordering a 3D print through a printing service and upload-ing to Thingiverse. If you have a Thingiverse account set-up, you may wish to upload the kids' projects to share their designs with library users and 3D enthusiasts around the world. If you are unable to print all your kids' designs at the club meeting and want to make it easy to find each club member's design, have the kids rename their design file. When you create a new object in Tinkercad, the program automatically gives your design a wacky and unique name. However, these names are not that useful when a group is sharing access to an account. Click on Properties and rename the file so it's easy to find later. You may wish to use each child's name and the date or any naming convention that makes it easy to find everyone's design later. You can also adjust the visibility of your projects. By default, all projects are Private, but you can change that setting to share with other Tinkercad users.

If you are working with a smaller group, you can have everyone working on the same design, such as you might do if using Project Ignite. And you could always remix the button lesson and have the group work with cube shapes rather than round shapes for the but-tons. One of the button options is a smiley face, so you could even challenge the kids to complete one of the button lessons and then see if they can figure out how to create a Minecraft creature button.

If you don't have a 3D Printer, you can still work with Tinkercad. Learning how to use the CAD program and getting into creating your own designs is at the heart of introducing 3D design and printing in a library program, as you want to get your club members bringing their own ideas to life rather than printing endless things from Thin-giverse. Tinkercad has the "Download for Minecraft" feature, which provides a great opportunity to introduce real-life skills and tie-in with the game. If your library does not have Minecraft accounts, walk the kids through the "Download for Minecraft" feature and show them how they can put their designs in their game at home.

When you are happy with your design, click on Download for Mine-craft rather than Download for 3D printing. You will then see a dialog box that asks you to set the scale by saying "Choose the size of your design in the blocky world." By default, it is set for 1mm=1 block. You can set the millimeters to be the size you wish or let the kids experi-ment with each particular design. Click on Export and your file will download to your computer. In order to put the design in Minecraft, you need to have the MCEdit program installed on your computer. You can find out more about the program and download it at http:// www.mcedit.net/. Once you have installed MCEdit, you can open the program and load the world you wish to put your design in. *One thing to keep in mind is that you cannot have both MCEdit and Minecraft open at the same time or it will not work.* To import your design, open the world in MCEdit and then click "6" to import. Choose your schematic file and click open. This puts the design in the editing world, where you can adjust the scale. Once you have the size you like, click "Ctrl-S" to save it, and then quit the MCEdit program. You should now be able to open your world in Minecraft and see your design in your world. There is a bit of trial and error involved in getting things just right, but you can go back and forth between MCEdit and Minecraft until you get things the way you want them.

There is so much more you can do with 3D printing, design and Minecraft. There are a host of free CAD programs you can try, so find the one you are most comfortable working with and using with your club. It's also great to combine the items you design or even things you find on Thingiverse with other Minecraft programming. You can print out creatures to use in storytelling activities, use 3D printed cookie cutters for other crafts or for making cookies, and create all kinds of projects using 3D printing as your base for other types of creations. Like Minecraft, there is a world of possibilities with 3D printing and design. Why not give it a try?

5

Minecraft and Literacy Activities

While many people strongly link Minecraft and computer games in general to the world of computer coding, the proliferation of YouTube Channels and books based around Minecraft help link the game not only to new digital literacies that are part of the world children live in today, but also to traditional literary activities.

STORYTELLING ACTIVITIES

When my club first started meeting, the library had many unexpected closings and late openings, due to snow and bad weather, making it difficult to plan really involved activities. Our club was just getting started and I was trying to figure out how it was going to work. Could we run activities that ran over several sessions? How do we deal with the new kids who show up at nearly every session? The same kids being there week after week were not something that seemed to happen at our location. How do I keep expenses down? These are just some of the challenges facing the club, and it's still an evolving process. Each "season," we have new kids join us and kids leave the club. Due to the location of our library—it's not in a walkable location, we're not near a school, and while we are located conveniently to the bus, the school bus does not stop at the library—I continue to explore new ideas and ways of running activities. Every library is different and what may work for one may be an abysmal failure for another. One thing that is constant, however, is that kids LOVE Minecraft. Now that Microsoft has purchased the company, many are wondering if this will be the end of the game, but from recent developments, it seems apparent that the company has big plans for this unexpected phenomenon.

So, getting back to the beginnings of our club, due to the crazy weather I had to really rethink some of my initial programming plans. I was finding it hard carving out time to learn how some of our newly acquired tools worked, and we did not have any staff who were familiar with it either. With no time to adequately prepare, I needed to come up with some low-tech but fun activities for the club. While trying to figure out what we were going to do in February, when once again I had no time to learn the Silhouette Craft Cutter, hype about the LEGO movie was starting to build. Then, unexpected news fell in my lap, giving me the perfect opportunity to introduce storytelling activities to the club! Stories began appearing in my Facebook newsfeed about Warner Bros. buying the movie rights to Minecraft and that Roy Lee, producer of the LEGO Movie, was onboard to produce it. If there is one thing I've learned from observing kids in the library is that Minecraft is about more than just gameplay. Fans love to talk about it, watch videos of people playing as much as they enjoy playing themselves.

At that first storytelling meeting, I just walked into the room with paper, pencils, and an idea to present to the kids: If you were to make a movie about Minecraft, what would you want it to be about? This opens the door to not only discussion and brainstorming about what kinds of things they would like to see in a Minecraft story, but also to introducing them to the different parts of a story and the process of thinking about how they would go about bringing that story to life.

There are many ways you can incorporate storytelling into a Minecraft in Real Life Club and into Minecraft gameplay. You can bring in-game elements, where participants have the opportunity to create their stories in Minecraft, you can introduce using film as a way to tell a story, and even have the kids write their own short stories or poems. Storytelling also provides a way to bring digital literacies into your club. In today's world, having an understanding of how the digital, online world works is very important. Digital literacy involves more than just having an understanding about how to stay safe online, it also incorporates the tools people use to tell stories in today's world. We see the stories in the news not only about newspapers and journalism having to evolve to keep up with the different ways in which people obtain news today, but also the same is true of traditional entertainment forms. TV is no longer the only game in town and younger people have moved online for their entertainment needs. One only needs to do a search for Minecraft on YouTube to see the endless options for viewers to get their Minecraft fix even when they are not playing the game. "Stampy Longhead," "Bajan Canadian," and "The

Diamond Minecart" are household names to young Minecraft fans. In 2014, Minecraft was the second most searched term on YouTube, only *Frozen* had more searches. Not only does Minecraft get a lot of views on YouTube, but also a whole toy line has been introduced based on their popularity. TubeHeroes are a new line of action figures and collectables aimed at tweens starring some of the most popular YouTube stars, including Dan TDM, Captain Sparklz, and more.

It's not surprising that YouTube videos took off as a form of entertainment for Minecraft fans. From the early days of the game, Notch and the Mojang team encouraged users to share videos of themselves playing the game. This was really a brilliant bit of no-cost advertising for the small game trying to get off the ground. Of course, no one could have imagined that it would become so huge. How big is YouTube viewership for the biggest YouTube stars? CaptainSparklz has nearly 8.9 million subscribers and is estimated to earn close to $1.6 million a year off his channel. Dan TDM (The Diamond Minecart) is at almost 8.5 million subscribers and his estimated yearly earnings are estimated to be between $658,000–10.5 million (Social Blade The Diamond Minecart 2015). At one time, Stampy was the most popular Minecraft YouTuber, and although that is no longer the case, his numbers are still impressive. He has more than 5.7 million subscribers and his videos have garnered over 3.5 billion views, putting him ahead of Lady Gaga for overall views. Stampy is so big that Disney hired him to create educational content for them and he has worked with Jack Black on his Internet series for kids. There are even websites selling t-shirts, pajamas, and lunchboxes featuring the biggest kid YouTube stars. Minecraft has become almost an industry in and of itself!

YouTube is not the only place where you can see Minecraft taking off as a way to tell stories and take the game into the real world. Have you ever run a search for Minecraft in Amazon or taken a walk in the game and children's sections of Barnes & Noble? You'll see Minecraft popping up in these places as well, not only in the form of guides to help you play the game, but also in the form of stories that create new lives and adventures of our hero, Steve, and new friends created out of the imaginations of the authors. While the authors of these books may not be superstars like their YouTube counterparts, these popular series and authors serve as further proof that fans are excited about anything Minecraft. Nonfiction titles, such as Scholastic's *Minecraft Construction Handbook* and *Minecraft Combat Handbook* are also unseating and surpassing big titles from stars like Jennifer Lopez and the *Guinness Book of World Records* on some of the bestseller charts (Groux 2014).

For those who prefer a story with their gaming, Minecraft Story Mode was released in October 2015. With great voice acting and a game company known for creating epic games behind it in Telltale Games, Story Mode is bound to be a popular edition to the Minecraft Empire.

Tying your library's Minecraft programming to literacy is a great way to make a connection to the more traditional library functions. Creating a literate community is one of the reasons libraries exist, and for the reluctant library director or board, connecting to this mission of the library offers a way to open the door to bringing Minecraft to your library.

While tying into literacy is an obvious direction for a library program to take, there are some unique challenges you may face when running a Minecraft IRL Club. You have to be prepared to deal with those kids who attend thinking they are coming to play Minecraft and not engage in other activities. It's an easy sell to parents, many of whom are looking for activities that engage their kids' interests but doesn't involve more screen time. For the kids, who may have not been given the full scoop by their parent or just stop reading after the word Minecraft in your publicity, you are going to have to figure out what you will say and how you will engage those kids. You may not only lose some of the kids who are disappointed that the club is not about playing the game, but you can also convince some of these kids to give it a try. Sometimes, one of the disappointed kids will continually bring up the issue and be difficult to engage because you are not playing the game. Be prepared for the reality that some of those kids won't come back and move on. Give kids the option of staying and trying out the activity, but make it perfectly clear that they do not have to stay. If they become disruptive, ask them to leave! It's always best to see if you can engage those kids in some way, but it's not worth disrupting your entire club meeting or spending the whole time dealing with that kid to the detriment of the majority of kids, who want to be there.

Many of these storytelling activities are too ambitious to complete in one meeting session. Depending upon the community your library is located in, this can present an additional challenge. When I first started planning this club, I envisioned a club that would include more continuity and building of skills from week to week. I thought I would have the same group of kids return week after week and we would have newcomers on occasion, but not at every club meeting. I almost immediately had to rethink my ideas about what the club would be about and how it would work, as it was clear that we would not operate in the same way an afterschool club at the Y or in a school would. If you are lucky enough to have a regular, returning group of club members, you will be able to take a different approach to the club since it will be easier to move into more advanced topics if you see the same kids meeting after meeting. So, if your club is like mine, you'll want to have the story ideas on hand so that you can easily integrate any newcomers into the activity.

Digital Literacy

Besides the basic literacy of learning to read and write, libraries today encompass more than just the basic literacy because life in the 21st century requires people to know more than just the basics. Today's kids need more than just how to read and find information if they are to grow into successful adults. Digital and visual literacies are now just as important to navigate the world as is the ability to read and write. You likely know and are familiar with basic literacy, but what about visual and digital literacy? Digital literacy is more than just being able to use a computer or search for Minecraft on YouTube. Digital literacy includes being able to interpret, evaluate, and create content, using what you find. How do kids use the information they find and how do they make educated decisions about what they find? Visual literacy includes more than just the ability to interpret what we view, but also the ability to create and communicate using visual means of communication. Visual literacy also can include an appreciation and sense of design and the ability to create or change what we see to craft a new piece of work. While you may think that today's kids are born possessing these skills, they are not. Much like reading and writing, these skills must be learned and Minecraft can help. What better way to learn than through something you love?

Minecraft, and the culture that surrounds it, offers many possibilities to help kids learn and hone these skills. As you can see, these activities not only tie-in traditional literacy skill, but also bring in those 21st-century literacies that are just as important to understand in today's world. They will not only sharpen their writing skills, but also work hands-on with the tools of visual and audio creation. They can share their projects not only with library users, but also to the wider world if you so choose.

Stop–Motion Animated Shorts and Moviemaking

iPads, tablets, and smartphones make it very easy for anyone to create a short film. There are a variety of simple-to-use video creation tools available for free or for a very low cost that make it easy to get started. There is even a creation tool just for creating Minecraft stop–animation films! These programs are a lot of fun because kids can dive right into creating their films without any prior knowledge of the app. They are very simple to learn and offer a great opportunity for the kids to explore and teach themselves how to manipulate the software to create a piece they are happy with.

Some good apps to get started with include:

- Minecraft Stop-Motion Movie Creator (iPad, iPhone, and Android) FREE
- iMovie (Apple only) FREE
- Stop Motion Studio Pro (App Store, Windows, and Android tablet/phones) $4.99
- LEGO Movie Maker (App Store Only)
- Microsoft Movie Maker (Windows PC)—this is a free and easy-to-use program to edit footage. Import your picture files into this software to create your video

There are several ways you can run a program like this. You can put out iPads or tablets loaded with the app along with LEGOs, Minecraft miniatures, and paper crafts, and let the kids just dive in and start creating their movies. Another way is to introduce them to some of the behind the scenes steps involved in the moviemaking process. A great way to do this is to introduce the idea of storyboarding. Whether it's an animated film or live action, storyboards are created to not only pitch the idea, but also to help visualize the storytelling process. Storyboards can be quite detailed, including a sketch to represent the action as well as description of the kind of shot they will use for the scene, music, dialogue, or whatever the filmmakers will find helpful in shooting a particular scene of a movie. There are some wonderful examples of the storyboard process available on YouTube to choose from or you can show examples of storyboards from popular shows like Adventure Time and Regular Show such as these:

- Adventure Time Story Board http://bit.ly/advtimeboard
- Regular Show Story Board http://bit.ly/regshowboard

If you know a particular movie or animated series is popular in your library, try to find a video of the storyboarding process for that piece. For example, Pixar is involved in supporting Maker Education and they love to share their process of creation. There is a wonderful short video, "Pixar Storyboard Mini Doc" (https://www.youtube.com/watch?v=7LKPVAIcDXY&feature=share), about storyboarding the Pixar way that is fun and informative and is great for getting across the purpose of storyboarding.

Once you have introduced the topic and storyboarding process, you are ready to dive into the heart of the program, creating animations. All tables are provided with storyboard templates to use (a good template can be found at http://bit.ly/mcstoryboard) or not, in generating ideas for their stories. During the filmmaking process, you will find some of the kids working together in groups, but some prefer to work alone. Unless someone seems lost and left out, let the kids work how they like. Because you may not always get the same group of kids from program to program if you are running this as a multi-part workshop, you may see one large group form from the kids who have participated in previous weeks—ask them to include any newcomers when they are ready to film. Some of the parents may also offer to stay and help out, and you may find some kids prefer to work with their parent or family members, as well. For a program like this, it is often to your advantage when this happens, as the parents get excited about the process and learn along with their kids. They may download the app to their phones and continue making animations at home once the program is over. Parents are often unfamiliar with many of these tools, and you may even find parents requesting classes for adults, which is definitely a great expansion of the Minecraft programming.

To encourage some brainstorming and idea creation prior to filming, place the LEGOs, miniatures, and other props and characters on tables around the perimeter of the room. If these things are on the tables where they start out, the kids get distracted by the toys and focus their attention more on the toys than on creating a story. Also, as mentioned earlier, placing the materials in a common place rather than at each table encourages more collaboration and sharing and allows the kids to see what others are creating.

If you don't have the budget to purchase Minecraft-branded toys or if you want to add other elements to your program, have the kids create their own characters and props. Creating short films can be a great culminating activity if you are running your program as a series. The kids might design creatures and props in a 3D printing and design program to use in their films. Creating the sets and props from cardboard or creating their own paper crafts is also a lot of fun. Often, the kids like to combine a variety of materials and commercial items to be able to create the story they wish to tell. When working with this kind of program, it's helpful to have a cart of craft supplies or be close to your supply cabinet so you can supply any last minute materials that kids are looking for.

At the end of any moviemaking program, be sure to collect email addresses so you can get the movies off the tablet and send them to the participants. You may wish to create a DVD of all the movies and give one to each participant, so they can see what others created and be inspired by each other. YouTube and Vimeo are other options for sharing your club's movies. A fun way to end a moviemaking series is to have a short film festival and invite the families in for a final viewing of everyone's creation.

Podcasting

Podcasting is a bit more ambitious of an activity to introduce to your Minecraft programming. It is a lot of fun, but requires more knowledge of recording software, and requires a bit more encouragement and facilitation to get the kids up and running with recording. This is also the kind of program that is probably best run as a series, as it would be very difficult in a 1–2-hour program to get to the point where you can write and record a podcast; but with the right group it can be done.

One of the best things about introducing podcasting to your group is that it is often a new concept for many kids. Minecraft podcasts are not nearly as plentiful as YouTube vlogs, so there is a lot more for the kids to learn and it introduces a new way of conveying information. You can make comparisons to their favorite YouTube stars, as podcasts often tell a story, review games or mods, and cover a variety of material. Creating podcasts introduces kids to a new way of transmitting information in a nonvisual way, which may be unfamiliar to them.

Elements of a Good Podcast

- Name for your podcast
- Logo
- Script
- Lead speaker or narrator

You don't really need a lot of sophisticated recording equipment or even a recording studio to do this. You can record using an iPad with Garageband. You can also work on a desktop or laptop computer and use the free audio recording software called Audacity (http://audacityteam.org/), or if you have Macs in your space, just stick with

Garageband. Both programs are easy to learn, in terms of the basics, and there are numerous tutorials available on YouTube as well as on Lynda.com, if your library has a subscription.

Lynda.com Tutorials

- Up and Running with Audacity with Garrick Chow
- Podcasting in the classroom with Erin Quigley
- GarageBand '11 Essential Training with Todd Howard has a section on Creating Podcasts

Helpful YouTube and Web Tutorials

- "How to Create a Podcast Using Audacity" by Vickie Siculiano http://youtu.be/J5P67TPlJ3U
- Free Audacity Tutorials.com has tutorials for beginning through advance techniques as well as recommendations on recording equipment. http://www.freeaudacitytutorials.com
- GarageBand Tutorial 2015—How to Record a Podcast with GarageBand https://youtu.be/BiNjUNNKvzE
- How to make a Podcast in GarageBand App (multi-part series) https://youtu.be/XKQu1hOeOw0

These are just some of the resources available to help you start learning about the various programs and apps available to get you started with podcasting.

At my club, we worked on podcasting over three sessions and I admit we never produced a final product. However, this was still a successful and worthwhile endeavor for our club. The kids worked together and honed some of those 21st-century skills mentioned previously. The podcast was a complete group effort, each participant contributed, and they voted on what things they wanted to include, on what the logo and name would be. Everyone had a chance to record and work with the software. So, at the end of the day, we may not have released a completed product, but the program was able to achieve all the goals we had set out to accomplish.

Introduction to Podcasting—Session 1

- Inexpensive composition notebooks or paper
- Examples of podcasts bookmarked or pinned for easy access (video game podcasts can be found at https://www.podomatic .com/trending/categories/Video%20Games)

If you'd like to try this approach, at the first podcasting session, introduce the idea of what a podcast is and look at some of the different topics that podcasts cover. Discuss what a podcast is and have the kids think about the ways podcasts are different from the YouTube videos they are familiar with. Give each participant a "podcasting journal." They will use this journal to write down ideas both at the club and to record any ideas they may have for the podcast between sessions. Encourage them to develop the ideas they come up with at home so they are prepared for the next session.

Once you have introduced the kids to a variety of podcasts, have them brainstorm ideas for a name for the podcast. Give them about 5–10 minutes to brainstorm, they can work on this independently or as a group. When time is up, go around the room and have them share their ideas. In our club, we voted as we went along and came up with a few good names after the sharing session. Once you have narrowed it down to a few good names, have a final vote to determine the name of the podcast. Our club voted to call our podcast "World of Minecraftia."

To set your club up for the next podcasting session, discuss the next steps that are necessary for creating a podcast to publish. Talk about logos and look at logos used by other podcasts or even the logos of their favorite YouTubers. Have the kids discuss their observations about various logos. Keep in mind that there may be size limitations depending on the publisher you use when we go to the design portion at the next session. Podomatic (http://www.podomatic.com) is a good, free resource for exploring and publishing podcasts. The size limitation for photos or logs is 600 × 600, so a basic design is best. When you click on a category to search the podcasts on Podomatic, the results are displayed with the logos, so this will help the kids get an idea of what the logos look like for a variety of podcasts. You can end the meeting by brainstorming ideas for the kinds of things the kids want to talk about during their podcast and what kind of podcast they want to record.

Introduction to Podcasting—Sessions 2 and 3

- iPads or Apple computer with GarageBand installed
- Laptop or Desktop computer with Audacity installed
- Microphone
- 5-channel mixer (optional; we use a Behringer mixer)
- Lightening to USB camera adapter (optional if using a mixer with iPads)

At the beginning of session two, review some of what you have done previously to catch up any newcomers who did not attended the previous session. If there is more than a week between sessions, this review is helpful to refresh everyone and get up to speed more quickly. Next, get to work on the Logo. Allow the kids to spend about 20 minutes working on logo designs, and then work to combine them into one unifying piece. If you don't wish to do that, have the kids vote for their favorite design, like you did for the Podcast title in the first session.

Next, get in to the hands-on recording piece. Our group had an iPad set up with a microphone as well as the laptop running Audacity. If you are going to record using an iPad, it's important to note that you will be plugging the microphone in using the headphone jack. This presents a bit of a problem, because in order to listen to your recording you will need to unplug the microphone, listen, and make adjustments, and then plug the microphone back in to record more. You can avoid this by purchasing a lightning to USB camera adapter and a small USB connected mixer, such as the Behringer 5-Channel mixer, to avoid having to do this back and forth. If you are recording with a desktop or laptop, this is not an issue, but you may wish to use a mixer as well because it can make things easier overall, and you can sometimes run more than one microphone at a time. If you can give the kids the opportunity to try out both methods of recording, you can then offer them a choice as to which method they prefer when it comes time to record the actual podcast. Give the kids time to experiment with recording and using the software so they are more comfortable when it comes time to record the podcast itself.

At the second and third sessions, you can spend time working out ideas for the podcasting and developing script ideas. Like the storyboard, the script is helpful for creating a good recording. If you have a script, even if you stray from it at times, your podcast will be more polished and you will have fewer moments of silence, umms, and other effects that result from the speaker, forgetting what they are going to say and that you don't want in the recording. One of the nice things about a podcast is you don't have to memorize the script prior to recording, since no one can see you. In developing our podcast, the kids talked about some things that they thought were essential to include for the audience. As the facilitator, you can help guide conversations like this by asking questions and getting kids talking. Depending on the mix of the group and their comfort level with each other, you may have to guide more of the conversation to keep them talking and thinking.

At the second and third session, give the kids the opportunity to work with the recording software. Be prepared for fear of the microphone. Some of the kids in my group were very shy about recording their voice and wanted to pass the microphone to the next guy as quickly as possible. All the kids who participated did record a small introduction saying who they are (first names only) and what they love about Minecraft. If you are working with a large group, you will likely find that the kids gravitate toward certain tasks that they enjoy, and they may even divvy up the different things that need to be done to create the podcast. Some kids may discover they like to write, and will therefore focus on the script writing process, while others may be drawn to the idea of being the "star" and will want to be one of the speakers, and still others may be more drawn to learning the recording and editing process. While it is great to introduce the kids to all parts of the process, consider letting the kids find their roles. Again, this ties in to the ideas that Tony Wagner has put forth that in developing 21st-century skills through hands-on learning—you can help kids discover their passions and interests.

Short Stories and Poetry

While technology and maker programs are a lot of fun, cultivating basic literacy is still a core function of libraries. Books remain a large part of our circulation and, lucky for us, Minecraft books represent an exploding category found on the shelves of bookstores and libraries. While these books may not make the best seller lists, there are some good series out there and they can provide another way to hook reluctant readers through something they are passionate about. One of the best of these is the Gameknight999 series of books that was released in 2014. You can use these books and even Minecraft Story Mode as a way to bring the idea of telling more traditional stories to your program.

There are many ways to use Minecraft to get kids creating and writing their own stories or poems. You can do it as a more passive program or as a creative writing series. Celebrate Poetry Month in April with a Minecraft poetry workshop or have the kids come up with their own Minecraft-inspired jokes and have a joke telling workshop. You can even bring in the digital world by introducing memes and having your kids create their own Minecraft memes. You can also work with the kids to create a book that can be placed in your library collection or even introduce your kids to the world of zines and create a Minecraft IRL zine. The idea is to engage young learners with language and storytelling in a fun way, honing their writing and storytelling skills.

An easy activity to get started with is to have group members create their own small books from a single sheet of paper. Once they have created their books, they can then work on creating a very short story or poem to fill the pages. Since this is a very short and sweet project, it is a great starter activity to launch a series of activities or a bigger story project.

Create a Book from One Sheet of Paper

Materials

- 11 × 17 inch paper of any color
- Scissors
- Markers, crayons, and pencils

Fold the paper in half by joining the 11″ sides to each other. Fold the paper in half again, joining the shorter ends once again. You will now make one last fold in the same manner as the first two folds.

Unfold the paper twice so that it is now half of its original size. Grab your scissors and make a cut, starting from the folded edge on the crease in the middle of the fold towards the center of the paper. Cut along the crease until you reach the center away from the fold.

Open your paper until it is completely unfolded. Now, you will fold the paper in half again to join the long sides of the paper. Pinch the edges of folded side of the paper, the area you cut will be in the center. Join the two edges together to make a "t" shape meeting in the center of the opening.

You now have four flaps of paper. Wrap any two of these flaps together and your book will form. You are now ready to fill with pictures and words!

Optional Stretch Activity—Use the circuit stickers and copper tape to add effects to your books.

Storytelling and In-Game Building

Due to the sandbox nature of Minecraft, the game can easily be used as a jumping-off point to introduce elements of story to your club members. As kids build their creations in the game, they often have a narrative in their mind as they build. They choose skins to personalize their character and bring that narrative to life through the things they build. Minecraft Story Mode was released by Telltale Games in the fall of 2015. Story Mode introduces a new main character, Jesse, and a host of new characters, sending them on an adventure to save the world.

The story plays out in a "choose your own adventure" type format where the player's choices guide the action. Even before Story Mode, players have been creating their own stories, though they may not realize that they are doing this.

Materials—Session One

- Paper, pencils, and markers
- Storyboard templates
- Video cameras (optional)

Introduce the activity by getting the kids to think about the elements of a story. Who is your story about, where does it take place, when does it take place, and last, what is it going to be about. Once they understand the elements that make up a good story, you can break the kids up into teams. These teams will work together to generate ideas and come up with a story that will be the basis for what they build together in the game. Breaking the kids up into teams makes it easier for them to come up with ideas, and also gives kids a way to get to know one another better.

Have the group spend one club session brainstorming ideas about their stories and working together to narrow the focus and incorporate everyone's ideas. This activity not only incorporates the traditional literacies, but also the collaboration involved has been identified as an important skill that people need to be successful in the future. You may wish to start off the first session with an icebreaker activity, but I have found that there is not much of a need for icebreaker activities in the Minecraft IRL Club. The kids love to talk about the game, so the initial activity is of getting them to start talking about story elements is really all you need to spark conversation amongst this group. If you have parents or other people to help out, it's a nice addition as they can help the kids stay focused and record the ideas as they come up. Although it's not necessary to have assistance, it can help keep things moving along and make sure the kids make progress with their stories. If you don't have people to help you run the club, just be sure each team has paper, pencils, and markers to keep track of their story and ideas. You will likely find that each group develops their own method for working out their story and each team member may take a different approach. Some of this depends on the age of the kids you are working with, but be sure to let the kids know before they start that either writing out the ideas or drawing their ideas is acceptable. You may wish to introduce storyboarding as part of this activity. It may be easier for the kids to work out their ideas in a more structured format offered by the storyboard. There is also less writing required when using the storyboard approach, making kids who struggle with handwriting more comfortable and able to get their ideas out. If you have video cameras available, you may wish to make them available for the kids to use to record their ideas rather than writing or drawing them out. Another option to do this is to have the kids come up with the Who, What, and Where of their story, and then have them start to bring together the plot through the storyboard.

At the end of this first session, collect all their story materials and place them in separate folders labeled with their team name, so they are on hand for the next meeting when they will have the opportunity to bring their creations to life.

Materials—Second Session

- Computers running Minecraft or Minecraft Education Edition
- Storyboards, written ideas, drawings from session one
- Graph paper
- Cardboard boxes, tubes, or whatever you have laying around
- Video camera

The second session will be eagerly anticipated by the kids because they get to build in Minecraft! At the end of the first meeting, where the kids worked out their stories and ideas, I collected all their materials and placed them in folders labeled with their team name so they would be on hand for the next meeting when they would have the opportunity to bring their creations to life. There are two reasons to do this—one is so that you don't have to start at square one at the next meeting because kids may not remember to bring back their papers. If you don't have the same group of kids every session, it is definitely important to keep the materials at the library so you don't have to start from scratch or rely on one child to bring the materials for the second session.

So, now the kids are ready to build their stories in Minecraft, but you still want them to plan what they are going to build before setting them loose. At this point, you will introduce the idea of prototyping. Talk with the kids about how engineers and designers prototype their ideas before starting the building process. This brings in more of those 21st-century skills that you are trying to build through your program. By having kids plan out what they want to build before they go into the game, you are helping them to refine their ideas, and also speeding up the building process since they will start building with an idea of what it is they want to build. If you don't have Minecraft accounts or computers available, this will be how they bring their stories to life to share with their fellow club members. Once the kids know what they want to build and have an idea of how they want to do that through their prototypes, they are ready to build in the game. This is an activity that you really need to monitor. You could also use a few helpers to ensure that everyone gets a chance to contribute and build. If you are running this on your own, circulate around to each group to be sure they are working together and everyone is getting a chance to contribute. Set a time limit for the build. Keep the teams updated on how much time they have left and remind them that they need to pick out one or two team members who will share with the club their story and what they built in the game. Once the build period ends, gather the teams together and get them settled down before going into the sharing process. If you can, connect a computer to a projector so that everyone can see the builds and have the teams come to the front of the room to share their story. If you can't do this, just be sure the kids understand that they need to be quiet and respectful to their club mates. This is also a great recording opportunity, so consider recording each team as they tell their story. It's great to be able to share these with the participants so they have a record of their creation, and you can also share it with parents and even the public if you receive written permission from parents or guardians via YouTube, Vimeo, or even on your library's webpage. You might even create another program with these stories and have the kids work with video editing tools to create a final piece of work.

As you can see, there is a whole host of ways that you can tap into the traditional and 21st-century storytelling methods as a way to not only encourage creativity, but also to build those essential 21st-century skills.

6

Minecraft and Making

Minecraft is a natural fit with the maker movement and with what informal educators, such as librarians and those hosting Makerspaces, are trying to accomplish with their programs for youth. Like Minecraft, the Maker Movement centers around trial and error, learning by doing, experimentation, and user-directed projects—those most important 21st-century skills that you are trying to build through programs. The library is a great venue for this type of programming, precisely because it is not a formal educational institution. The public librarian has no curriculum they need to follow, there are no tests, and we want the kids to have fun while learning something. As mentioned earlier, in schools, the Makerspace is often found in the library as schools and school librarians navigate the new landscape we all find ourselves in. The passion kids have for Minecraft can be leveraged to build skills that will serve them well throughout their life, long after their interests move on to other areas.

Maker activities bring Minecraft into the real world at your library. There are many inexpensive tools for exploring circuits and even programming through more concrete, hands-on activities. One of the great things about the game is that you can explore a variety of topics in the game without having to worry about real-world restrictions. Things like physics and the rules of circuits do not apply, although there are also some restrictions that are unique to the items found in the game.

Redstone is a tool in Minecraft especially suited to bring learning into the real world. In the game, Redstone acts as a circuit of sorts, but there are rules and limitations placed on this special tool that make it act differently in the game than a circuit works in real life. While maker activities explore more than just circuits, much of the following section focuses on ways to incorporate learning by using circuits to bring Minecraft into the real world.

EXPLORING CIRCUITS WITH MINECRAFT

Soldering Sunday, part of the FUBAR (Fair Use Building and Research) Labs located in New Brunswick, New Jersey (http://fubarlabs.org), has created a kit that will really help you get into exploring how circuits work in the real world, including switches, buttons, and more. The kit, called "Minecraft Circuits in Real Life," is a great way to explore this area, no soldering or special skills required. Instructional videos are provided to help you work with the kit before introducing it to your group. The kits include small breadboards, a battery pack, LEDs, switches, buttons, resistors, and any other components you need to work with from creating basic to more complicated circuits. If you like to include gameplay in your club, these kits offer you a great way to introduce a concept in real life, and then set up an in-game build challenge using the concept just learned.

Soft Circuits and Minecraft

While the "Minecraft Circuits in Real Life" kits can be used to introduce the topic, you can also use e-textile or soft circuit projects as another way to work with circuits. E-textiles, sometimes referred to as soft circuits, combine sewing projects and circuits to create clothing, toys, or other items that light up, make sound, interact with the environment, or more. The great thing about introducing circuits through e-textiles is that your group can make projects that they can take home. Start with a simple circuit, lighting up one LED and work your way through parallel circuits, adding effects with a small preprogrammed microprocessor called LilyTiny and basic coding to add effects with the LilyPad, an Arduino-based microprocessor that you program. You can either set up a series of workshops that work through various projects to build skills, or simply pick and choose projects you are comfortable starting.

   If you are working with younger kids or you are not sure what kind of sewing skills your group possesses, start with a simple project that requires less sewing, although there are always work arounds if you want to focus more on the coding aspects. However you proceed, make sure you are not introducing anything that requires too many skills the kids do not have—you don't want to discourage them by starting at a level that is too advanced. Sometimes, what seems simple to us is difficult for the kids, and sometimes difficult to predict. I have found over the last few years of running library maker programs that a project I may think will be too easy or boring, but after 15–20 minutes is actually very engaging for the kids.

If a lot of kids attend your program on a regular basis, you will get to learn what engages each one and get an idea for how they work. In any group of kids, you will see that some kids get very involved in the design process and enjoy the artistic aspect of figuring out what they want their final project to look like, laying everything out, and experimenting with different ideas. Other kids are more interested in getting the project completed, caring less about the design and more about "will it work?" If you have enough helpers, you can plan an expansion of the project for those who finish quickly and are looking to learn more, or consider having some extra materials on hand so they can make a second or even third project.

The Torch Book Light is a very simple project and offers a great entry into the world of soft circuits. This item is easy to make, requires minimal sewing, and can be done for a low cost—an important criteria for a Minecraft IRL Club operating in a public or school library, where budgets are always a concern. The great thing about this project is you can expand it beyond the book torch project. If you have kids with more advanced sewing skills, or if you want to build these skills, consider having the group create small felt Creepers, Endermen, or other Minecraft cube creatures with eyes that light up or blocks that glow. Taking it a step further, add a LilyTiny element, where Minecrafters can add an effect to their creations and learn how to add additional lights, which make the project a bit more complex. If you are really ambitious and your budget allows, you can even teach some basic Arduino programming using the LilyPad to create an interactive project. Let's get started with the first and most simple e-textile project, the Minecraft Torch Book Light.

Minecraft Light-Up Torch Book Light

The Torch Book Light is a great place for your club to get started learning about circuits through a project they can take home. This project can easily be completed in one 90-minute session. Let's start by taking a look at how to introduce and run the actual workshop, followed by the directions for creating your own. In this workshop, you will start by introducing a very basic circuit.

Start the workshop by getting the kids to think about how Redstone works in the game and talk about things they have built in Minecraft using Redstone. You may find that some kids who attend your club do not play Minecraft or they have not built with this particular resource. However, like Star Wars, Minecraft is one of those things that kids know about whether they have actually played the game or not. By getting the kids talking, they can make that initial connection to something they are familiar with in the game and it's a good way to introduce the element to those who are less familiar with it.

Once you have talked about Redstone and circuits in the game, it's time to introduce a very basic real-life circuit. Everyone is given a red or yellow LED as well as a 2032 coin cell battery. Ask the kids to make observations about the light and the battery—what do they see, do they know what LED stands for, and more. The kids will probably notice things like the two legs of the LED light being different lengths, the battery is flat, and that the battery has a + on one side. Be sure to ask the kids questions and make them feel comfortable answering, even if their observation is not relevant or they give the wrong answer. The idea you always want to keep in mind is that the kids drive the program and the conversation. Making these observations ties into the activity where they will need to be able to identify the + and − connections of the LED and on the battery holder.

The kids are now ready to create their first real-life Redstone circuit. This is a fun workshop introduction I learned from Paul Gentile of Soldering Sunday and is a fun way to learn the basics and make the Minecraft connection. Have them put the LED on the battery, with one leg touching either side of the battery. Some kids will have their light go on, but others may find that their light does not light up. This is another point to ask them questions about why this may be so. Have the kids whose light did not light, try again. They should then realize that they need to flip the LED so that the long leg is touching the positive (+) side of the battery. Then, have them go back to their previous observations about the battery and LED to make the connection that one side of the battery is positive (+) and one side is the negative (−). They should also come to the conclusion that the LED legs have a positive (long leg) and negative (short leg) connection. This is important not only for learning how circuits work in the real world, but also for realizing success in their projects.

Before starting to build, summarize the lesson by explaining how the circuit works. The battery stores energy, producing voltage or the potential for the electron to do something like light up our LEDs. Electric current flows from positive to negative in a closed circuit and the LEDs are designed to work this way, as well. Thus, the energy flows from positive to negative making the battery pass energy to the LED causing it to turn on. Because electric current flows from positive to negative, the LED will not turn on if the positive connection of the LED is not connected to the positive side of the battery. You can explain this visually by drawing a picture on a whiteboard or even illustrate the concept through a circuit diagram. A circuit diagram is a schematic drawing illustrating an electronic circuit and its components. These diagrams are used by hobbyists and engineers to help them design actual circuits. The ability to read a circuit diagram is an important skill for more advanced projects, so tying them in early is a great way to build skills. Once you are done with the explanation of this basic circuit, hand out the materials for the project.

Once everyone has their LED, battery holder, and conductive thread, have the kids make observations about each item. You may wish to have magnifying glass on hand, as it may be difficult for some kids to see the + and − symbols on the LilyPad LEDs used in this project. Ask them what role they think the conductive thread plays in the project. The thread conducts electricity, carrying energy from the battery to the light across a distance. They need to remember that, like in the simple circuit they just created, the positive sides must match up. So, they need to find the positive side of the battery holder and sew to the positive side of the LED, repeating this step for the negative connection.

The kids can now get their felt pieces and think about how they want their project to look. They can play around with the pieces and plan out where they would like to put the battery holder and LED. When working with soft circuits, it helps to have the kids sketch out the circuit on paper before they sew. For a project like this, it's less important, but it's a good practice to introduce now, as it becomes more important when you start adding more LEDs, a LilyTiny, or LilyPad.

Next, introduce the straight stitch and show the group how to attach the thread to the felt.

For e-textiles projects, you should have at least one or two people to assist with running the workshop. This is especially important if the kids do not have experience with sewing. You can take some shortcuts to keep things moving, such as having all the felt pieces cut out in advance, pre-threading the needles with conductive thread, and putting all the materials needed for each participant in a Ziploc bag. You do not need to limit the project to being a torch, you could have felt available in a variety of colors and the kids can create their own book lights, perhaps making a creature or block found in the game. If you have kids who easily complete the project with one LED, consider having other options available so that they can experiment with adding additional LEDs to their project.

Now that the kids know what the project is and have been shown the basics of attaching the battery holder and the stitch that they need to complete their project, they are ready to start assembling the torch. The kids will probably take longer to sew than you anticipate, but this is ok. They are learning a valuable skill—not only in learning how circuits work, but also acquiring simple sewing skills. There may also be more troubleshooting involved than you may have initially thought. Help the kids find the solution to "my light doesn't work" by guiding them through the process. It's important that any volunteers you have helping know what kinds of questions to ask to help the kids come up with the solutions to the problem themselves. Asking things like "what do you think happened?" or "what things do we know about circuits?" can help get their minds working toward a solution. Avoid telling them exactly what to do, if possible. Some of the things to look for to help you facilitate include:

- Did they match the positive and negative connections?
- Is their sewing very loose (if their stiches are too loose, it can interfere in the flow of electricity)?
- Is the thread loose at the connections?
- Are there any areas where they crossed connections or is the thread touching the other connection when you connected the LED or holder to the felt?

The kids will be pretty pumped when they get their projects to work and they will be eager to tackle more advanced projects. It's a lot of fun to get boys sewing and excited about something like e-textiles, which is often seen as a stereotypical "girl" activity. At the same time, e-textiles are attractive to a lot of girls, so this project can be a great hook to attract girls to your Minecraft programming if you find this to be a challenge in your community. This activity is a bit challenging, is a great skill builder, and brings about great satisfaction when you have that "ah-ha" moment that occurs when a switch is turned on and the LED lights up.

MINECRAFT TORCH BOOK LIGHT

The Torch Book Light is a very simple project that is a great entry into the world of soft circuits or e-textiles. This project is easy to make, requires minimal sewing, and can be done for a low cost—an important criteria for a Minecraft IRL Club operating in a public library where budgets are always a concern. The Torch Book Light is a great place for your club to get started learning about circuits through a project they can take home. This project can easily be completed in one 90-minute session.

The Torch is something that any Minecraft fan will recognize. The torch is a basic but necessary item in the game. If you are to survive your first night, you will definitely need to craft a torch to ward off Creepers, Zombies, and other creatures of the night in Survival Mode. Torches will light your way as you dig down or light a Jack O' Lantern. It's something every player learns how to craft early on in the game, so the kids will definitely be familiar with this item.

Once you have completed this basic soft circuit project, you are ready to introduce more advanced projects. Soft circuit projects are particularly appealing to girls, so if you are trying to attract more girls to your STEAM programs, this is a great way to go. Future projects can introduce parallel circuits—the LilyTiny and then the LilyPad.

Skill Level—Beginner

Kids will learn the basics of circuits. They will learn how to sew a simple straight stich and attach items to a sewing project in the same manner you would with a button.

Materials

- 2032 coin cell battery
- LilyPad Coin Cell Battery Holder with switch (Sparkfun DEV-11285) or Sewable Coin Cell Battery Holder 20 mm (Sparkfun DEV-08822)
- 1 Yellow (Sparkfun DEV-10047) or Red LilyPad LED (Sparkfun DEV-1044) or 5–10 mm yellow or red LED
- Conductive thread (Sparkfun DEV-10867 or DEV-11791)
- Sewing needle and needle threader
- Felt—brown, dark brown, yellow, orange, and white (you can pre-cut these to save time, template included in the back of the book)
- Felt glue or embroidery floss, depending on how much sewing you wish to incorporate
- Paper and pencils

How to Make a Minecraft Torch Book Light

1. Create a template to use for the book light. You can either precut all the felt pieces or provide templates to the kids for cutting. You can also have them sketch their design and circuit on paper, and then cut out the pieces.
2. If the kids have drawn their torch designs on the paper, they can use that template to design their circuit. Have the kids design their circuit on paper by figuring out where they wish to place their LED, where they want the battery to be, and then drawing their circuit paths. It's important to remember to mark the positive and negative connections on the LED and battery, and be sure the circuit lines do not cross (if using the switched battery holders, you only need to sew a connection from one positive and one negative).
3. Cut out the paper pattern and trace it onto a piece of brown felt. Trace and cut out the square and rectangular pieces from the other colors of felt that you wish to include in your project.
4. Using felt glue or liquid stitch, glue on any pieces that you wish to include on your torch before sewing the circuit. You can glue pieces on after you have completed the sewing as well; it just depends on how you would like your finished design to look.
5. If using standard LEDs, you will need to prepare them in order to sew them onto your project. With a Sharpie or any other kind of marker, mark the positive lead leg so you can identify it later. The positive leg is always the longer one. With a pair of needle-nose pliers, grab the end of one leg of the LED and twist carefully into a spiral shape. Repeat with the other leg. Make sure your positive leg is marked in a place where you will be able to identify it when you are ready to sew the light on.
6. Attach the battery holder to the felt by placing a small dot of the glue to the back; this will help hold your battery holder in place while you sew. Now, thread your needle with the conductive thread and attach to the backside of the holder to secure it to the fabric. To securely attach the holder, pull the thread through your fabric, leaving a half-inch to 1-inch tail. Hold the tail with your finger and pull the thread through the fabric again to make a loop. Take your needle through the loop and pull tightly to make a knot. I like to go through a second time to make an additional knot to be sure it won't come undone while sewing. This step is probably the most difficult for the kids, so you may have kids asking for help with this.
7. Pull the thread through either the negative or positive hole on the holder. Repeat this one to two times more as if sewing a button to keep the battery holder in place. Using a straight stich,

sew from the battery to the light making sure that you follow your circuit diagram and sew your path to the matching polarity on the LED. Once you reach the light, sew through several times to make the connection. Make a knot of the backside of the fabric in a similar fashion as you did with the battery holder to secure the light. Cut off the remaining thread, making sure you don't leave a long tail that could come into contact with the thread from the other side of the light.

8. Repeat steps five and six to connect the opposite side of the battery to the LED.

9. Insert your battery into the battery holder and turn on the switch (the LED should come on when inserting the battery into the non-switched holder). The LED should illuminate if everything is attached correctly.

10. If you LEDs light up, you can add any additional features you wish to your project. You may wish to add a backing to your light by gluing or sewing another piece of brown felt to the back, which can be decorated or left blank. If the light does not turn on, troubleshoot the issue and get your project working before adding any finishing touches.

Troubleshooting

I've completed my sewing but my LED doesn't light up. What do I do?

- Check to be sure that the polarities match—positive sewed to positive and negative to negative.
- Is your thread sewn on tightly or is it loose? If the stitches are loose at any point in the project, your light may flicker or not stay on.
- Did you cross your "wires"? If you did not sew in a straight line from the battery to the light but crossed your threads, your project will short out and the LED will not light. Make sure that your lines are not crossing or touching. Be sure to check the tails where you attached the light and battery holder to be sure they are not too long making contact with the other part of the circuit.
- If all else fails, try a different battery.

Other Things to Try

1. Don't want to make torches or want a more open-ended project? Have the kids design their own Minecraft Light-Up Book Lights. Provide a variety of colors of felt so they can create Mobs, Steve, Alex, or anything else they can think of.

2. Have the kids figure out a way to create a switch for the unswitched battery holder.
3. Introduce parallel circuits if you are working with teens or a group with more skills. If you have kids that have attended other workshops and have an understanding of circuit basics, let them experiment with adding more than one LED to the project.

LILYTINY, LILYPAD, AND MORE ADVANCED PROJECTS

If you want to continue to explore e-textiles and circuits, you are ready to introduce multiple LEDs and LilyTiny elements to your group. The LilyTiny is the first step to getting into the more complicated world of the LilyPad. The LilyTiny is a preprogrammed microcontroller that allows you to add effects to your e-textile project. A LilyTiny has four effects available—twinkle, blink, heartbeat, and fade—as well as negative (–) ground and positive (+) connection. A Minecraft creature plush or block is a relatively simple LilyTiny project. Since sewing may still be a hurdle for your group, you could also have the kids use a commercial Minecraft plush and add light up elements to it. Once you get into adding more than one LED or a microcontroller, it is important for the kids to plan out their project on paper before they start sewing. If they do not plan their circuit in advance, they may find that not only does their project not work, but also they may find in the middle of sewing that they cannot complete the circuit as they thought they could; they have to remove all their stiches and start over. For kids who try to take shortcuts, this can offer a valuable lesson of learning through trial and error. Moving up to adding LilyTiny to projects is a great way to add interest and build skills without having to know how to program the Arduino-based LilyPad.

If you have more time or want to get into a more advanced soft circuit project, introduce the LilyPad. The LilyPad is an Arduino-based microprocessor designed to work with e-textiles. While it is more complicated, it opens the world of more advanced maker projects outside of e-textiles to your group as they learn to program the LilyPad in Arduino. A fun and relatively easy project for introducing the LilyPad is making felt pillows or creatures. A project such as this can be completed in three to five 90-minute sessions, depending upon the skill level of your group. You can spend one session programming the LilyPads and the remaining sessions focused on designing and creating the project. This project can add an interactive element by bringing in conductive fabric. The LilyPad can be programmed to activate the program when the fabric is touched. You can find an outline with code to complete the creature/pillow project or a t-shirt at http://www.technigals.org/#!workshops/cgeu. These directions were used in a project at the Middletown Free Library called TechniGals and can easily be adapted for use in your Minecraft e-textiles programs.

More Circuit Activities

Some of the most popular maker activities are those that center on using and learning about circuits through different materials and activities. Redstone is the cornerstone of creating intricate builds in Minecraft and understanding circuits is essential to many maker projects. Like Redstone, circuit activities can be simple additions to handicrafts and can be accomplished by adding an LED to a project. Or you can introduce more advanced ideas and even use it as a gateway to basic programming.

If sewing is not your thing, not to worry. There's no need to get more complicated than you are comfortable with. There are a lot of fun and easy projects you can do with basic circuits, and I find that the kids who attend maker programs in the library never tire of making things light up.

CONDUCTIVE ART

Building circuits is one of those activities that you can return to time and again. Kids never get tired of making things light up and come to life. A fun way to incorporate circuits into your club is through art using materials that can conduct electricity.

Paper circuits are another way to explore how circuits work in the real world. If you have an artistic group or if sewing is too difficult for your kids, this offers a great alternative to soft circuits. Inspired by artist Jie Qi, paper circuits use copper tape, coin cell batteries, and LEDs to make art, greeting cards, or origami come to life. If you have a group that is passionate about Minecraft Paper Crafts, this is a great way to add a twist to just creating Minecraft characters and blocks. While you can use standard LEDs in paper circuit activities, I have found circuit stickers, or chibitronics (http://chibitronics.com), to be an easier and attractive way to bring your projects to light, if your budget allows. Circuit stickers are specifically designed to be used in paper circuit projects and are easy for your younger makers to use. Paper circuits are a lot of fun and are a less expensive way to combine art and circuits than the e-textiles projects explored in this chapter. The chibitronic website offers a learning page that can help you get started with your first circuit to more advanced techniques.

Perhaps you don't like the look of the copper tape or you have club members that are passionate about adding effects such as sound and music, LEDs, and more to their projects. Conductive paints and pens are great tools to explore and have endless possibilities. I highly recommend purchasing a starter kit and exploring these materials before introducing them to a group. In my experience, paper circuits have a very low rate of failed projects, as they are simple, easy to work with, and easy to troubleshoot. Due to the nature of inks, there are more variables when you're working with pens and paints, which tend to cause more areas for failure than the paper circuit projects.

Whether you go with paint, stickers, or ink, you can add things besides LEDs to your projects. Chibitronics (circuit stickers) have add-on components that allow you to add effects similar to the LilyTiny, including blink, fade, twinkle, and heartbeat. Sensors are now available that can really add excitement to your paper circuit art. The chibitronic sensors include a light sensor, microphone, and a timer circuit. The Circuit Scribe includes components such as switches, potentiometers (a kind of adjustable resistor that allows you to adjust the power that flows to the output), buzzers, and sensors. You can also add components to conductive paint projects as well as expand your options with the Bare Conductive Touch Board.

The Circuit Scribe is a rollerball pen that uses nontoxic conductive ink and can be used to draw your own circuits. Electoniks (http://www.electroninks.com/), the company behind this product, has teamed up with AutoDesk to give you a way to prototype before you draw out your circuits. The web-based AutoDesk app 123D Circuits (http://www.123dapp.com/circuitscribe) is one way to introduce circuit design to your club members. The app runs in a web browser and makes all the components for the Circuit Scribe available to you, so you can begin prototyping and planning circuits.

Although you don't need to use the 123D Circuits app to use the Circuit Scribe, there are some advantages to using it. The app allows you to not only plan out your design, but you can run a simulation to see if you have everything set up correctly without having to waste any ink, paper, or other materials. A single pen costs $19.99 as of this writing, so conserving ink is something you want to consider. Once you complete your project design in the app, you can save it as a PDF and print it out. This is an easy way to introduce the concept, have the kids trace the circuits, and see it come to life. It builds confidence and allows them to get a feel for the pen or the ink before starting their own designs. As the club facilitator, you can also design a sample project for the kids to work with before having them move on to their own designs.

Bare Conductive paint can be used in a similar way to the copper tape you use with the circuit stickers. The conductive paint comes in a tub that you paint on with brushes as well as a pen similar to a glitter glue pen. Depending upon the ages of the kids you are working with, you may find one type is easier to use than the other. I have found that kids often have a hard time controlling the amount of paint that comes out of the pen and often end up using way too much. It is easier to control how much paint you are applying when you use the paint brush and a small tub of ink. If the ink is too thick, you can dilute it with a little water, keeping in mind that the more you dilute it, the less conductive it is. In order for the circuit to work and light up, the ink needs to be mostly dry, so it's important not to apply too much to the project. Like the conductive pens and the copper tape, you can use the ink in a variety of projects, but since you can paint on the circuit, it makes it easier to increase the scale of your projects.

What library does not have an excess of cardboard boxes lying around? Why not create Minecraft-based costumes and add a conductive paint element to it? Besides lighting up LEDs, Bare Conductive sells something called a Touch Board. The Touch Board allows you to turn conductive surfaces and materials into a sensor. It includes an onboard MP3 player, making it easy to add sound to your projects. So, you could use it to bring Note Blocks into your club projects, as the Touch Board can work as a MIDI synthesizer, and it can send MIDI signals to a laptop or iPad running Abelton LIVE. You can also use the Touch Board on its own or you can introduce programming to your club with the Arduino interface. What makes Bare Conductive so great is the number of possibilities it offers, and the fact that you can grow projects as your skills and comfort level, with these kinds of activities, grow.

LITTLEBITS AND MINECRAFT

littleBits offers you another great item to bring into your maker activities. littleBits can be used for a variety of projects and activities; it's amazing the ways people have adapted these for use in a variety of settings. littleBits was founded by Ayah Bdeir in 2011 when she sold her first kits. The idea behind littleBits is to cut out the barriers that designers, artists, and engineers face when they want to prototype or create a project. These easy-to-use circuits can bring elements of design thinking into your programs, as well as creating a challenge for the kids to work with.

littleBits snap together with magnets and take out the added steps of soldering or coming up with the electronic components your creation may require. They are color coded and it's easy to learn how to use them, allowing you to spend your time perfecting your creations rather than getting bogged down in all those other tedious tasks. littleBits is growing by leaps and bounds, and they are always adding new bits and collaborating with other makers, creating more programming and project possibilities available.

Like Minecraft, littleBits are a tool with an easy point of entry. You don't have to know more than this:

- Blue Bits = power
- Pink Bits = input
- Green Bits = output
- Orange Bits = Wires (or extensions)

The best way to run a program with littleBits is to introduce the kids to the bits and give them some time to play before diving into a project. Once they've had a chance to play and explore, maybe 15–30 minutes, they are ready to dive in and create. littleBits gives you another entryway to exploring Redstone and circuits, or you can take it in a totally different direction. The beauty of littleBits is that the possibilities for what you can do are endless.

Using littleBits to explore Redstone allows you to combine IRL activities with in-game activities. This activity will explore creating circuits and creations using Redstone in the game, and then trying to recreate those creations using littleBits.

REDSTONE LITTLEBITS CHALLENGE

Materials

- Computers or laptops running Minecraft or MinecraftEDU
- littleBits (26–126 modules, depending on program size)
- Nine volt batteries
- Scrap paper for brainstorming

For this activity, set up two stations. The first station is a littleBits station and the second station is comprised of laptops running Minecraft or MinecraftEDU. At the littleBits station, the kids build a Redstone circuit using the bits, and then move to the Minecraft station to recreate the circuit in the game using Redstone. You can reverse this order, or if the number of computers or bits available is an issue, have some kids working on building in Minecraft and the others working with the bits. Make sure everyone has scrap paper to keep notes or drawings of their circuits so they can recreate it when you switch stations. You could have the kids work individually or in teams. It's important to set a time limit for each part of the workshop. Be sure to keep the kids updated as to how much time they have left to work. Facilitating this activity involves keeping track of time and keeping the kids on track so they at least create a basic circuit.

As part of the Global Chapter program, littleBits has been running monthly challenges focused on a theme that usually ties in with holidays, seasons, more. A challenge workshop can take a variety of forms, but it's always a great way to introduce newcomers to your club and to littleBits. If you have a lot of new participants who have not worked with littleBits, start with an exploratory bits activity, which you could tie-in to Minecraft or not. For example, you could do a Minecraft Bits Scavenger Hunt as an icebreaker and bit exploration activity. Take a variety of bits and put them in a box on each table or split them into groups and give each group a box of bits. In this activity, the kids will explore the bits in their box and think about related items in Minecraft or in real life. For example, they may have a button and LED in their box; can you create something using these bits in Minecraft? Be sure each box includes a power bit and battery, so that the participants can experiment with the bits and get their ideas going. Give the kids about 15 minutes with this activity, and then bring the group back together to talk about their observations and thoughts about the activity. Once you have given the kids a chance to share, you are ready to introduce your Minecraft Challenge. The Minecraft Challenge can really be anything that you can think of and think will be challenging, but is not too hard for the kids to come up with ideas and create. Base your challenge activity around the bits and kits that your library owns, bring in other materials such as cardboard, straws, craft materials, LEGOs, and others to use alongside the bits. Some challenge ideas include having the kids create an IRL Minecraft game, a Redstone contraption challenge, Minecraft storytelling, or really anything you can think of would be great. The idea is to get the kids thinking—by using their creativity, working together to come up with an idea, and figuring out a way to make it come to life.

bitCraft is one of the latest collaborations that littleBits has announced. bitCraft is a mod designed by littleBits with the goal of combining the fun of playing Minecraft and inventing with littleBits. To get started with bitCraft, you will need the following bits:

- Cloud Bit
- USB Power Bit
- Slide dimmer
- Bar graph
- Minecraft account
- Technic Launcher (download available at http://technicpack .net/download)
- littleBits bitCraft mod installed via Technic Launcher

This is all you need to get started to learn how to use the Cloud Bit and experimenting with bitCraft. littleBits has created a world that you will see when you launch the modpack called "Welcome to bitCraft." This world is a great entry point to use not only to learn about the Cloud Bit yourself, but also as a way to get started inventing with bitCraft and the Cloud Bit. This world will introduce you to the Cloud Gateway, a special "block" that represents the Cloud Bit in Minecraft. In this special starter world, you will learn how to craft a Cloud Gateway, as well as walking you through two additional rooms where you will learn how to connect the Cloud Bit to the Cloud Gateway and how to set the direction the commands will flow. You can either Transmit information from the Cloud Gateway in the game to the bits you have set up in the real world or Receive, which will send information to the Cloud Gateway from an action you take using the bits in the real world via the Cloud Bit.

You can use this in a program by combining Redstone Circuit Challenge activity and an introduction to bitCraft and the Cloud Bit. littleBits has partnered with popular YouTuber, Dan TDM (The Diamond Minecart), to create a couple of videos introducing bitCraft. As Dan TDM is so popular, showing one or both videos is a great way to get started. The videos can be found on the littleBits bitCraft webpage at http://littlebits.cc/bitcraft. If you have multiple Cloud Bits, you can have the kids work together to move through the Welcome to bitCraft world. If you don't have multiple Cloud Bits, you can work one-on-one or two-on-one with the kids and take them through the first three challenges in the Welcome world while the other kids are working on the Redstone Challenge. One thing to keep in mind is that the Welcome world does not reset itself, so you may wish to use multiple accounts to work through the world, have the kids log in with their personal accounts or have them go back to the previous rooms and just have them destroy and rebuild what was there. Since these are very simple and basic introductory activities, this is not a big deal and will not take up a lot of time. Since this was just launched recently, I have not had time to experiment with it too much, but I am very excited about the possibilities of this for Minecraft in Real Life Club programming.

MAKEYMAKEY

The MakeyMakey is described as "an invention kit for the 21st Century." It was invented by Jay Silver and Eric Rosenbaum, based on research at MIT Media Lab, where they both worked with the Scratch programming language. Like so many new inventions, it was launched as a Kickstarter, and they recently ran another Kickstarter for the portable MakeyMakeyGo. The MakeyMakey connects to your computer via USB and can turn just about anything that can conduct electricity into a controller making the computer think you are using a regular keyboard or mouse. To use the MakeyMakey, all you need to do is connect it to the computer and then, using alligator clips, attach one end to the MakeyMakey itself and the other to the object or material you want to use to control the mouse or keys on the computer. As with any kind of circuit, you also need to be sure to ground yourself, which you can do very simply by connecting an alligator clip to the ground labeled as "Earth" on the MakeyMakey, and then clipping the other end to yourself or hold it in your hand.

The MakeyMakey allows kids to connect the physical and virtual worlds of Minecraft, and it gives you a great way to put all that cardboard lying around your library to good use! The MakeyMakey can hook up to objects to control the arrow keys, spacebar, mouse click, as well as a, s, d, w, f and g keys by hooking wires up to the spaces on the bottom. You could even have the kids design Minecraft tools, and then connect them to the MakeyMakey to control that tool in the game, or create Redstone-controlled items that are triggered in-game when someone steps on a pressure plate, flips a switch, or pushes a button that they created in the real world.

If you have kids who are interested in getting into coding and you are up to the challenge, the MakeyMakey easily partners with Scratch. Scratch (scratch.mit.edu) is relatively easy to learn, and "snap" programming language is a good entry point to programming for kids.

There are many books and even free online courses through Coursera and edX that can help get you started. Just remember, you don't have to be an expert, keeping one step ahead of the kids is enough to be able to guide the activity and learning. The kids can create their own games and animations using Scratch, create their own controllers in the real world, and then combine the two.

SQUISHY CIRCUITS

Squishy circuits are probably the easiest way to explore circuits and can be used successfully with preschoolers, school-age children, and teens. Squishy circuits are a fun and inexpensive activity that you can use in a variety of ways. Squishy circuits allow you to create circuits and circuit art using play dough. Squishy circuits came out as a project at the University of St. Thomas's Playful Learning Lab, with the idea of creating activities and tools that would allow kids of all ages to explore circuits. Anyone can create circuits using this dough, which makes a great entry into the real world of circuits!

Squishy circuits have two parts—a conductive dough and an insulating dough. The dough has conductive properties that allow it to act as a wire carrying the electric current from the battery to the LED, motor, or even a buzzer. The insulating dough is important if you are going to create conductive squishy art. The insulating dough has no conductive properties and it prevents the current from passing through. Commercial play dough is conductive, which means it can be used in a Squishy circuit activity. If you have a hot plate, you may wish to have the kids make the conductive dough as part of the program. You do not need to cook insulating dough, so if you want to make dough, but don't have access to a stove or hot plate, you can have the kids make this dough and either pre-make your conductive dough or provide play dough. Once you have the dough ready, you can get into a more creative activity.

MINECRAFT CREATURES SQUISHY CIRCUIT ACTIVITY

Materials

- Conductive dough or Play-doh in a variety of Minecraft colors
- Insulating dough (plain or add food color to make colored dough)
- LEDs in a variety of colors
- AA batteries and battery holder with wires
- Motors and/or buzzers (optional)

For the Dough

- Water
- Flour (regular or all-purpose gluten free)
- Salt
- Cream of tartar or nine tablespoons of lemon juice
- Vegetable oil
- Food coloring
- Sugar
- Deionized or distilled water

In this activity, you will have the kids work in groups to make the conductive and insulating dough, and then create Minecraft creatures or blocks that light up having moving parts or make noise.

For the insulating dough, mix one cup of water, one and half cups of flour, three tablespoons of cream of tartar (or nine tablespoons of lemon juice), one tablespoon of vegetable oil, and food coloring in a medium-sized pot. Cook the mixture over medium heat and stir continuously until it forms into a ball in the pot. Once the ball has formed, carefully remove the ball of dough to a lightly floured surface. Let the dough cool for a few minutes before moving to the next step. Once the dough is cool enough to safely handle, have the kids take turns, or break into smaller pieces so each child has dough to work with, and knead it with a small amount of flour until the dough reaches a consistency you like. If you would like to work with more than one color, make dough in the various colors you need for the project. If you are having the kids make the dough, they can choose the colors, having each team make different color dough. Another option is to have the kids make one color of dough and have premade or commercial Play-doh available to supplement with. If you do not wish to make the dough as part of the program, either premake the dough in the colors you wish to use or just use Play-doh.

While a group of kids make the conductive dough, another group can prepare the insulating dough. The insulating dough is not made using heat, so you don't need to worry about providing as much supervision. For the insulating dough, mix one cup of flour, half cup of sugar, and three tablespoons of vegetable oil in a large pot. Mix in the deionized or distilled water a small amount at a time, approximately one tablespoon each time you add water. If the kids are making this dough, one child can be stirring while another child measures and adds the water. Continue adding water a tablespoon at a time until most of the water is absorbed into the dough. You will mix in no more than half cup of water and the dough is ready when it reaches a crumbly consistency. Once you have gotten the water mixed in, remove the dough from the bowl and knead it into one big lump. You will knead water into the dough until the dough has a sticky texture. Once you have a sticky dough, you will knead the remaining flour into the dough until you reach the texture you desire. This dough can be stored in an airtight container for several weeks. If you make the dough in advance or want to reuse it, you may find a condensation on the dough; just knead the dough a little bit and it will reabsorb this condensation. While you may color this dough, it is a good idea to keep your insulating dough white so the kids know exactly which dough is conductive (color) and which is insulating (white). Once you have all the dough made, the kids can start creating Minecraft art that lights up, buzzes, or has movement.

Minecraft Raspberry Pi and Programming

One of the things kids really like about Minecraft is the number of ways that people have customized the experience through Mods. Mods, or modifications, are new worlds that include games or help you create your world to appear in a different way. Unlike Resource Packs that limit the player to customizing the appearance of their world, a mod is much more powerful, in that it can change not only the appearance of the world, but also changes the way the game behaves. There are mods based around movies such are Star Wars or Tron, TV shows like Adventure Time, and even mods that add creatures that do not exist in the official version of Minecraft. Due to the open nature of the Minecraft game, it is easy to access the tools for creating your own Minecraft Mods.

Providing instructions for doing this are beyond this book's scope and the author's capabilities. However, there is a great educator resource available called LearnToMod (http://www.learntomod .com/), which you can use to introduce this area of programming to your club. Much like Scratch, it's a building block-based programming tool that makes for an easy entry into getting started and building basic skills. There is even a class on Coursera called "LearnToMod for Educators" by the University of California, San Diego (https://www .coursera.org/learn/learntomod/). This six-week course is self-paced and will have you exploring the wider world of Minecraft in education as well as getting you started with LearnToMod as an educator and using the curriculum they have made available. If you are at all interested in using this resource in your library, this Coursera class is probably the best resource to get you up and running.

The Raspberry Pi offers another way to go, if you are interested in programming with your club. The Raspberry Pi is a small, inexpensive computer that can be used not only for standard computing, but for creating a variety of projects as well. Unlike the Arduino, which is a simple microprocessor that runs one program over and over again, the Raspberry Pi is a computer that can run an operating system. Most Raspberry Pis run the Linux operating system, but the latest model is able to run Linux or Windows 10. If you are looking to get into more complicated programming or creating projects that can perform multiple tasks, then the Raspberry Pi is the way to go. It is also a great choice for libraries that would like to get into coding and are looking for an inexpensive entry point; they even have a $5 version called the Pi Zero. It's a full-fledged Raspberry Pi that can run Scratch, Minecraft, and other applications.

The Raspberry Pi version of Minecraft, called Minecraft Pi, is an easy way to get into coding with your club. In Minecraft Pi, instead of building using the keyboard and mouse, the player uses a Python interface to manipulate the Minecraft world. Python is a widely used programming language that is great for beginners, because it was designed for readability and to use fewer lines of code to execute the program than a language such as Java. Raspberry Pi Foundation is an educational charity that is based in the United Kingdom. The foundation's goal is to advance computer education for people of all ages around the world, and their website (http://www.raspberrypi.org) is the best place to start if you are looking to incorporate the Raspberry Pi into your library Minecraft programming. Just type Minecraft into the search bar and you'll get results offering you everything from introductory tutorials for getting started with Minecraft Pi to activities you can use with your club.

If the idea of installing the Raspberry Pi operating system (Raspbian or NOOBS) is intimidating, you'll be happy to learn that there is a Raspberry Pi made especially for kids called Kano, which makes it even easier to use the Raspberry Pi to teach programming. You can purchase a Kano kit and the kids can put together the Kano Raspberry Pi in a very easy, step-by-step process, or you can just download the operating system from their website (http://www2.kano.me/down loads) and install it on your own Raspberry Pi. Going this route is more expensive than simply purchasing a Raspberry Pi, but Kano is a fun way to get started so it's worth considering if you have the budget for it. The mission of Kano is to get kids to learn coding, so they offer a lot of great tools. The Kano version of Minecraft uses block programming like Scratch, so again it's an easy way to get kids started with code.

If you are looking for an even easier way to bring coding into your Minecraft club, then you will want to check out Hour of Code. In December 2015, Mojang teamed up with Hour of Code making an introductory Minecraft coding tutorial available (https://code.org/mc). Hour of Code's mission is to get kids coding and have computer science become a part of every school's curriculum. The Minecraft Hour of Code tutorial introduces the basics of programming logic in a fun way using block program. The young programmer works through the world as either Alex or Steve, and each lesson builds upon the one before becoming more difficult as you move through the module. At the end of the lessons, you can continue to explore and build using the knowledge just acquired. The great thing about using the Hour of Code lesson is that you do not need to have any experience with coding. It takes about an hour to work through all the lessons, so you can easily complete this yourself before using it with your group. This is also a great way to get parents working alongside their kids and introducing them to some of the educational benefits of the game.

While 3D printing may be the first thing that comes to mind when people think of Makerspace and making, you can see that it's so much more than that. By using Minecraft as a springboard to maker activities, such as e-textiles, Raspberry Pi, and paper circuits, you are laying the groundwork for the kids to branch out and explore other projects. Minecraft is a great way to turn kids on to other maker activities and get them excited about creating their own projects.

7

Crafting with Minecraft

While 3D printing, working with circuits, and podcasting are fun activities, we shouldn't forget about the other things that we've been doing in the library for some time now, and that includes more traditional craft program. If you are not comfortable diving into more technical activities, crafting offers you an easy place to launch your club. You probably already have many of the supplies you need in your library and it's fun to just create with more traditional materials. Traditional arts and crafts can be just as much a part of making and the maker movement as more high-tech activities.

MINECRAFT IRL CLUB AND DIY.ORG

If you are looking for ideas to help get you started or want to throw in badges for your club, be sure to check out DIY.org. DIY is a website for kids that allows them to explore a wide variety of topics, learn skills, and share their creations with each other. My 10-year-old son likes to call it Facebook for Kids, but it's much more than that because it's designed to encourage kids to do things in the real world that help them learn new things and develop new skills. It can be a great way to teach digital smarts in a safe environment, and parents can keep track of what their kids are sharing and see their progress as they work. It also gives the kids a way to create a portfolio of their work. You can set up a hashtag for the kids to use that will make it easy for them to find each other's projects. You can also set up a Minecraft IRL DIY Club or just use the site for ideas. If you are interested in a club, there is a handbook to help get you started. The club guide can also give you a great place to get an idea of one way to set up a Minecraft IRL Club, and ways to give the kids leadership roles and guide direction of the club in your library. Of course, it really depends on your community on how well this kind of set up works. If you have a club where you get the same kids for just about every meeting, you can do different things than if you don't get a consistent turn out and you have a lot of newcomers every meeting.

Some of the DIY badges that a Minecraft IRL Club can earn:

- Architect
- Cardboarder
- Cartoonist
- Game Designer
- Graphic Designer
- Minecrafter
- Super Fan

There are many other badges on the site that you can look at to find inspiration for projects for your club. You can tackle a badge at a time and work on the requirements at each meeting or just use the site to help you come up with ideas. A nice feature to consider, if you have the funds, is to award the physical badges as the kids earn them, or perhaps you can set up a way to award them on a bulletin board or create some other way to recognize your club members.

CRAFTING WITH MINECRAFT

Minecraft Food

Want to add a delicious twist to your Minecraft club? Why not create Minecraft-based food creations. The Internet is loaded with examples of Minecraft food for parties, cakes, and any number of occasions. One of the easiest ways to bring food-based creation into the library is by using Rice Krispie Treats. You can either buy premade treats or make your own, depending upon what is available to you at your library.

Minecraft Food and Movie Program

- Two pounds Rice Krispie Treat Sheet (or you can use the smaller or homemade treats)
- Canned frosting (or make your own) in green and white
- Tubes of writing icing in various colors
- Movie—*Mojang: the Story of Minecraft* from 2Player Productions
- Or playlist of kid-friendly YouTube videos

What better way to wind down the year or cool off on a summer day than with a movie? Movies need snacks, so why not make your own? For this program, the large Treat Sheet is perfect for cutting into square shapes for moviegoers to decorate in Minecraft style. You can make this a food only program by having the kids make their own Krispie treats, and even making their own icing. You can also tie-in the importance of measurement and some food science with this program to add those STEM elements that so many are trying to incorporate into library programming.

If you don't have the means to make your own treats, have the kids decorate using premade icing and using the premade treats. Once everyone is happy with their creations, take some pictures, and then sit back and enjoy the movie! If you want to show *Mojang: The Story of Minecraft*, there are a few things to keep in mind—this is not a movie made for kids. The DVD has a family friendly track which is great, but I would highly recommend prescreening it to be sure that you are comfortable with it for your library. (There were still a few lines that skirted the borders of family friendly in my mind.) If the audience for your Minecraft program runs younger, you may want to choose some kid-friendly YouTube videos instead of the movie.

Kid-Friendly Minecraft YouTubers for Younger Kids

- Stampy (Stampylonghead or Stampy Cat) is great for younger kids
- iBallisticSquid is also good for younger kids. He is Stampy's best friend.

Kid-Friendly Minecraft YouTubers for Older Kids

- TheAtlanticCraft
- The Bajan Canadian
- Maricraft
- Captain Sparklz
- Dan TDM—The Diamond Minecart

Minecraft Cardboard Creations

Cardboard creating and Minecraft were just meant to go together which is great for libraries since most of us have loads of cardboard waiting around to be reused and remade into something new! At the Middletown Free Library, we are always using cardboard for some kind of program—everything from Cardboard Roller Coaster challenges to mashups with littleBits and more. Cardboard is a great material, precisely because it can be used in so many ways and is pretty sturdy, so your creations will last for a while. So, what kinds of Minecraft projects can we use cardboard for?

Minecraft Tree

- Square (or as close to square as possible) boxes in various sizes
- Construction paper—brown, green, yellow, white, and a variety of other colors
- Tape—permanent scotch tape and duct tape
- String of holiday lights
- Scissors

Why not liven up your library with a Minecraft Holiday Tree? I found this to be a great family program, as the moms and dads had just as much fun creating our tree as the kids did. To make the tree, have your group figure out which boxes will make a good trunk and which will make good branches. We crafted one box to look like a torch for the top of the tree. The group then used the paper to decorate the boxes by taping the colored paper to the outside of the boxes. We stacked them up and used more tape to hold it all together. We then strung the lights, using clear permanent tape to hold the lights in place where necessary. Because we did this as a holiday program, the kids wanted to make presents for under the tree. They decorated a few more boxes to place under our Holiday tree. This is a great, easy, and low cost holiday program that anyone can do! If a Christmas program isn't right for your library, you could do this any time of the year and string up white lights or leave the lights off completely.

Global Cardboard Challenge

Every October, the Imagination Foundation holds its Global Cardboard Challenge. The challenge and foundation were inspired by Caine's Arcade. Caine is a boy who created an elaborate cardboard arcade in his dad's auto parts store in East Los Angeles. This inspired a filmmaker named Nirvan Mullick to create a short film about the boy and his arcade after becoming his first customer. Mullick went on to found the Imagination Foundation, which is a nonprofit, with the goal of fostering creativity and entrepreneurship in children through creative play. One of the great things about their program is that they are working to reach a global audience, and strive to make it easy and affordable for anyone to participate in their programs. The Global

Cardboard Challenge is a great way to do this, and you can create your challenge around Minecraft.

The Challenge is easy to run and the particulars are flexible. You can kick off in September, and then on the World Day of Play have people bring their creations to the library for others to see or play with. Another way to host a Global Cardboard Challenge is to host building days leading up to the challenge, when kids come in and work on their projects that will be revealed in October. Last, you can host an all-in-one event on or around the World Day of Play where you issue the challenge, have all the materials ready for creating, and then have everyone share their projects at the end of the day. If you want to officially participate in partnership with the Imagination Foundation, visit their website to register your event. The website, http://card boardchallenge.com/, provides you with everything you need to run your own challenge, including a materials list, official playbook, and a link to the Caine's Arcade film to show at your event for inspiration and to tell the story. When they first started, the Imagination Foundation chose a theme and asked global participants to work around that theme, but as the program has evolved, they have moved away from that model. So, now you can create your own theme or challenge for your event.

If you don't want to tie-in specifically with the Global Cardboard Challenge, you can always run your own Minecraft-themed cardboard challenge as part of your club. You could have cardboard costume challenges, Minecraft tools, Minecraft mobs, and more be the theme to center building around. The DIY Cardboarder skill is a great place to get inspired about using cardboard to build and create with.

Minecraft Holidays

Make your holidays even more fun with a Minecraft twist! Here are a few ideas for combining holiday celebrations with your Minecraft IRL Club:

Halloween

Looking to bring Halloween into your club activities? Nothing says Halloween like the iconic Jack O'Lantern. Why not have the kids carve pumpkins inspired by their favorite Minecraft characters? I know that many may worry about safety with such a program, but this can be done safely with guidance and rule setting from the beginning.

I've had children using Dremels, soldering irons, and drills in my space, and I cannot tell you how exciting this is for the kids. Many children do not get the chance to work with tools, so it's great if we can offer some opportunities to do so in a safe and controlled environment. Whenever I do a program that involves a tool or something that can be potentially dangerous, I begin with a safety talk. Anyone who wishes to participate in the program must arrive on time and be there for the safety talk. The kids must wear safety glasses and agree to be safe, meaning not only will they handle the tools as they have been shown, but also there will be no running, fooling around, or any other behavior tolerated that could cause a safety concern. In order to use tools in your programs, you need to be strict about the rules. I also have the kids and parents sign a waiver (safety, video, and photo) and safety agreement when they participate in any program that is part of our Makerspace. In the safety agreement portion of the form, they agree to follow all the rules, as well as agree to help keep themselves and others safe. For this program, I would also advise against purchasing the pumpkin-carving tools that you see in Target and other mass retailers. The cutting tools are very flimsy and could pose a danger due to their poor quality. I highly recommend the Quikut Safe Cutter for use in a pumpkin-carving program at the library. These are sturdy and cut through the pumpkin easily. Once the kids have carved their pumpkins, they can take them home for Halloween night or you can decorate the library with their finished creations. We added littleBits with a motion detector and Bright LED bit in ours, and placed them at the circulation desk. If you are decorating the library, be sure your program is within a week or so of Halloween to avoid the pumpkins getting moldy inside or rotting on your circulation desk. When you are ready to take them down, you can remove the littleBits and wipe them down to reuse in other projects.

There are many other ways to combine Halloween and Minecraft IRL activities. You could have a Minecraft costume challenge or contest, create a Minecraft-style haunted library, decorate bags for candy, or more. Be creative and ask your club members how they would celebrate Minecraft Halloween for more ideas and to really put them in charge of guiding the direction of your programming. It's always great to go to the source, especially if you are not a player yourself.

Christmas

A great way to create a Minecraft Christmas is to have your club create their own Minecraft Tree, and then create decorations for the tree that they can bring home for their own tree! These ornaments do not have to be for Christmas—they can be for other holidays as well, so kids who don't celebrate Christmas can still participate in this program, if that is an issue for you.

Supplies for Glitter Ornaments

- Clear cube ornaments (I used one and three-fourths glass ornaments I found on Amazon)
- White glue
- Glitter
- Glitter glue
- Permanent markers
- Glitter craft tape

Give the kids options as to which materials they want to use and offer a variety of decorating supplies, if it's in the budget. If you want to keep expenses down, you can leave out the glitter tape, as that is the most expensive item on the list and probably not one you already have lying around. One of the nice things about the glitter ornaments is that the glitter is inside the ornament which cuts down on mess in the library and at home!

To make the glitter ornaments, put a small amount of glue inside the ornament. Swirl it around a little so that it is not all collected in the bottom. Pour your glitter inside the ornament and swirl the ornament around to cover the entire inside of the ornament with glitter. This can take a while to get the entire inside covered with the glitter, so a little patience is required. We also had some kids make these using glitter glue rather than glue and glitter separately, which works as well. Once the ornament looks the way you want, add features to the outside using permanent markers or the glitter tape. Some of the kids used the glitter tape on the outside of the ornaments to decorate rather than the glitter glue method. Supplying a variety of materials is always a good way to go, as it provides means to experiment and allows the kids to create their own unique item rather than everyone making the same item.

Valentine's Day

Valentine's Day is another holiday which easily lends itself to Minecraft craft creations. The kids can make cards or Valentine's mailboxes for school. These projects can be very simple, using templates already available online or you can make them more complex by adding circuit stickers, making pop-up cards, or having the kids just create their own unique cards with markers, pencils, and crayons. Because some kids can be sticklers for detail, you may wish to print out templates in advance and have some pages bookmarked so they can be easily accessed during the program. That way, you can easily print out the ones the kids want to use for their projects.

MINECRAFT POP-UP CARDS

- Cardstock in a variety of colors
- Craft knives or scissors
- Ruler
- Glue
- Markers or crayons

Pop-up cards appeal to a wide audience because they can be fairly easy to make, or you can make more intricate and difficult cards.

For a basic pop-up, you need two pieces of paper that you fold in half. Put the color you want for the outside of the card aside and work with your inside piece for the pop-up. On the outside folded edge, find the center of the card using the ruler and make a small mark. From the center of the card, measure out 2 centimeters on each side of your center mark. At these two points, measure another 2 centimeters out toward the outside edge of the fold and make a cut to the 2 centimeter mark. Now, you are ready to open the card and push in the piece you just cut. Create or cut out a small picture that you want to pop-up when the card is opened. Glue this to the tab you just created. Decorate the rest of the card and it's ready to go! Once you are comfortable with this basic pop-up card, you can get more creative and create shapes that will pop up when the card is opened.

MINECRAFT VALENTINE TEMPLATES

These are some great sites for printing out designs for Minecraft Valentines. Some of the sites feature wrappers to place on candies, whereas others are more traditional card templates.

- BE MINEcraft Valentines Candy Wrapper Printable—http://club .chicacircle.com/be-minecraft-valentines-candy-wrapper-printable/
- Over the Big Moon Free Printable Minecraft Valentines—http:// overthebigmoon.com/free-printable-minecraft-valentines/
- You've Been Framed Free Minecraft Valentine Printables—http:// youhavebeenframed.blogspot.com/2014/01/im-no-creeper.html

- Creative-Type Dad Free Minecraft Valentines—http://creative types.blogspot.com/2013/02/free-minecraft-valentines.html
- Joe Cridge's Pop-up card templates (including a Creeper)—https://www.joecridge.me/2015/09/06/pop-up-card-templates/

Minecraft Paper Crafts

Paper crafts are a very popular IRL activity for kids who love Minecraft. I remember my son being so excited when the official Minecraft Paper Craft kits came out. These kits can now be found pretty much any place you can find Minecraft toys; and I really like them for making paper crafting easy, especially if I'm combining this activity with movie making or another program. These paper crafts are sturdy and easy to put together and they are not too expensive, as they will last a long time and can be reused for various projects.

Another great way to incorporate paper crafts is to have the kids design their own paper crafts. This can be easily done if you have tablets and a printer available in your library. The Minecraft Papercraft Studio is an app that is available for iOS, Android, and Kindle devices for a small charge of $2.99. This is an official Mojang-endorsed Minecraft app. Some of the nice features in this app include the ability to import skins from Minecraft accounts as well as the ability to print blocks, capes, and items. This app allows users to create custom models that they can then print out and glue together for unique paper crafts. You can also combine this app with the Minecraft Skin Studio to customize skins for turning into paper crafts. Like the Papercraft Studio, there is a small charge of $2.99 for the app. This is a great go-to program when you don't have a lot of time to plan a more complex program or you are looking for a passive program that you can set up in the library for kids to explore on their own.

Minecraft Building and Character Programs

Walk into the Minecraft section of any toy store and you'll see a variety of Minecraft action figures. There are mini figures as well as larger size figures representing the various mobs, characters, animals, and other creatures found in the game. Having the kids create their own miniature characters is a fun and easy craft program. You can use a variety of materials to run a character craft program, depending upon your budget and tools available.

Polymer Clay is a great material to explore for making miniature Minecraft characters. It's easy to work with, and you can find a lot of inspiration with a quick Internet search for various styles and techniques for working with the clay. A popular style for Minecraft polymer clay creatures is the Kawaii style. Kawaii is a Japanese term for cute, and is often associated with cute drawings and animation of food styles. Of course, you don't have to stick to a style, but if you are looking to make a sample or introduce a more structured activity, there are a lot of examples and YouTube video tutorials that can help you get started. When running this program, consider posting some examples from a Google search on your screen to give the kids some ideas, but have them create their own designs. If you are working with Polymer clay, you will need a toaster oven or access to an oven to bake the clay once the design is completed.

Another great material to work with when creating Minecraft creatures, blocks, and other characters are Project Bricks. These are bricks made of Styrofoam that can be cut, glued together, and then painted to create just about anything you can think of. They are great not only for making characters, but are also a great way to bring into the real world a similar type of building as is done in Minecraft. You could easily combine a Project Brick activity with a storytelling activity or have the kids build something with the bricks, and then see if they can recreate that building in the game.

LEGO bricks are probably the most familiar and popular building block around. The LEGO company has collaborated with Mojang to release official Minecraft building sets, which allow you to recreate the game in the real world. While these sets are nice, the whole point of Minecraft is the sandbox building with unlimited possibilities. So, I have some mixed feelings about these sets, but like any other LEGO set, there are the cool mini figures that are great for stop–motion animation programs and the kids just love them. One thing I do like about these sets is being able to have a collection of bricks that keeps with the Minecraft color scheme. They are mostly just boxes of bricks without all those specialty pieces that other themed sets have because of the nature of Minecraft itself.

LEGO is a great real-life tie-in activity, and there are a variety of ways you can use them in your programming. One thing you might like to do in a LEGO building program is to have the kids compare what it's like building with the LEGOs versus in-game building. With LEGO, you have different shapes and sizes of bricks available to create with, but you still have some limitations such as not having spheres or a large variety of shapes available to you for building with. If you like to combine some in-game activity with the hands-on offline activity, have the kids prototype a design in LEGO, and then see if they can recreate it in the game.

Minecraft, Pixels, and Pixel Art

One of the things that I often hear adults say about Minecraft is that they don't understand a game with such bad graphics having such appeal to today's youth. Many compare the game to the 8-bit graphics of the Atari games they loved as kids. While Minecraft may appear to be graphically unsophisticated, don't be fooled. Minecraft is a 3D Java-based game and can run in 32- or 64-bit, depending on the version of the game and your operating system. There are endless arguments about the processing speed versus the graphics, and many people assume the blocky graphics and the 8-bit style mean the game is less sophisticated than it really is. In fact, the retro feel of the graphics is one of the things that is appealing about the game for kids and adult players alike. The familiar block style building and pixelated style is part of what fuels the imagination. The blocks can be anything you want them to be, opening the door not only to creating impressive structures, but also for creating 8-bit style artwork within the game. This style opens the door for your club to explore what pixels are and of course the endless possibilities for creating 8-bit Minecraft-inspired art.

A great place to start any 8-bit or pixel art program is to see if the kids know what pixel is. Pixel is short for picture element and the more pixels that are in a picture, the more detail you will see. If you zoom into any image, you can see the pixels that create that image. The more bits available in a program, the more colors available (there is a great, short video that TeamKano has put together explaining what a pixel is at https://youtu.be/rf3_ZW2pJhk). While pixels do not have to be square, they always look square on computer screens. Pixel art is often created digitally and is created at the pixel level, meaning that the art is created pixel by pixel. Pixel art has become a popular style today due to the popularity of Minecraft, as well as because of a bit of nostalgia for the early days of video games. When the early console and computer games were created, the memory on those early machines was very limited. In fact, the phone you carry in your hand today holds more memory than early computers and video game consoles! In order to create a playable game, designers had to make sure the programming and art did not use up so much memory that the game was unplayable. Thus, the 8-bit style was born, but as computer memory became less expensive, the graphics and programming improved. One of the great things about Pixel Art is that it's easy for anyone to get into. You don't have to be a great artist to create art in this style and you don't even need a computer! There are ways to create the look of Pixel Art through hands-on projects.

Post-It Note Pixel Art

Creating Pixel Art with Post-It Notes is a great way to get the kids creating and decorating your library at the same time. For this program, use the larger square size notes along with the smaller rectangular shaped ones for added interest and for working in smaller areas. Pixels are sometime rectangular in shape, so it's not cheating to add these in, even though we are most familiar with the square shaped pixel. Have the kids preplan their ideas using graph paper to work out their design in advance. This gives them a plan to work from and helps cut down on waste when putting the projects together. This is a really fun activity and the kids love seeing their designs in the library windows and on the walls and bookcases. We did this on the library floor during library hours and it was one of the quietest Minecraft IRL club programs. Most of the kids worked on their own creations and were scattered around the library putting their projects together.

Pixel Art Mosaics

Pixel Art is very reminiscent of the mosaic art form. Both use squares to create an image. While mosaics can be created out of non-square found materials, most people are familiar with the art created using small square tiles. You can introduce a more traditional mosaic method with your group using wood as a base and ceramic or glass tiles to create designs. Some companies also sell coaster molds for creating mosaics, which will work as well. If that is too difficult, expensive, or time consuming, create paper or foam mosaics. You could also create mosaics using round, colorful candies, such as Skittles or M&Ms, to create designs. These are fast and easy ways to introduce this art form. Last, you can also do a mosaic project using LEGO baseplates and bricks to create your designs.

Tile Mosaic Materials

- Four- to six-inch wooden base
- Mosaic Indoor Stone Cement (comes in 2-pound tubs, need 2 tubs for 12 projects)

- Half-inch (12 millimeter) glass or ceramic tiles in assorted Minecraft colors—I like the color assortments at Mosaic Art Supply (http://www.dickblick.com/products/roylco-mosaic-paper-squares/)
- Grout—this comes in many colors and you can choose whatever color works with the project
- Spatulas to apply grout
- Clean sponges and warm water

Working with tiles is a two-step process that you need to complete over two sessions. The cement usually requires about 24 hours to dry before you can grout. For grouting, use the spatula to spread the grout over the entire surface of your project. Let the grout set for about 20 minutes, and then clean away the excess with a sponge and warm water. Your project is complete!

Paper Mosaic Materials

- Cardstock cut in a square shape for the base
- Precut or a variety of construction or cardstock paper pieces
- Glue

Foam Mosaics

- Wonderfoam Mosaic Tiles and Foam, cardboard, or any other base to glue tiles to
- Wonderfoam Classroom Mosaic Tile Kit—contains enough materials for 12

For a craft like this, the kids don't need to sketch out their designs in advance, as they can play around with the tiles to figure out their design. Once they have their design planned, they can then begin gluing the pieces into place. It is best, though, to have a template that they can work on so they can move their tiles one by one from the template to the project base.

Perler Bead Pixel Art

Perler Beads offer more possibilities in creating pixel art style designs with your club. Perler Beads can be found in just about any craft store and are very easy to work with. For activities involving Perler beads, you'll need the peg board to place the beads on to create your design, ironing, wax, or parchment paper as well as an iron set to medium heat. Like other projects, the kids can create their designs in advance on graph paper or by experimenting with the beads on the peg board. There are many templates that can be found on the Internet, as well. If you have limited time or peg boards, using precreated templates can save time, but you will sacrifice the creative piece of the program.

Perler beads can be used to create simple projects, but you can also get more complex creating 3D objects as well. Besides your basic design, you can expand the project to create a useful item such as a keychain. To create a keychain, create your design and after you have ironed it, poke a hole carefully through one of the beads on the perimeter of your design, then attach the keyrings jump bead through the hole. Another fun way to use Perler beads is to create a 3D Minecraft block and add a light-up element to it. An inexpensive and easy way to do this is to purchase battery-operated tea lights to place under the block.

3D Minecraft Perler Bead Block

- Perler beads in various colors
- Large peg board (you can use smaller square boards)
- Iron
- Parchment, wax, or ironing paper
- Battery-operated tea lights

Plan your design on paper, and be sure to leave every other space blank around the perimeter so that you can snap your project together. Be sure to pay attention to how you want to put the block together and plan your perimeter bead spacing accordingly. You will make five pieces altogether—the top and four sides of the block. Make each side of your project as you would any Perler bead creation. After you iron each side, place a book or any heavy object on top of the piece to ensure that it will remain flat. This is an important step to ensure that your pieces will snap and stay together. Once all the pieces are cool and have been flattened, assemble your block by snapping the pieces together according to your initial plan. Turn on the tea light and place it under your completed block, and you are done!

MINECRAFT AND OTHER REAL-LIFE CONNECTIONS

If you have followed some of the ways educators are using Minecraft, you already know that the game can be used to explore and engage kids in a variety of topics and subject areas. Minecraft is being used to help kids learn history, improve their math skills, and more. There are ways for libraries to make these connections in fun and informal ways that work in library spaces.

Minecraft, Building, and Architecture

Architecture is a great real-world Minecraft connection. One of the first things a player must do in survival mode is build a house. Kids and adults alike are recreating any number of architectural landmarks in the game and also designing all new buildings of their own. In fact, there are even architects making the links between Minecraft and architecture. The University of Southern California's School of Architecture and the USC Game Innovation Lab partnered to create a free, open-source game to crowdsourced city and urban planning. They cite such games as Minecraft and SimCity as inspiration, with the idea of letting anyone try their hand at urban planning, especially the people living in the city. In addition to collecting data from the designs submitted, the designers of the game see it as a great education tool to help people develop systems thinking, one of those skills much needed in the 21st century. Architect Bjarke Ingels was inspired by Minecraft and has created the theory of "Worldcraft," which focuses on turning "surreal dreams into inhabitable space." Ingels believes that architecture should use the same principals as Minecraft, and open architecture to the public to allow them to transform their own spaces and environments. He sees Minecraft as a place where there are millions of people using play to create and inhabit their own worlds. He says, "These fictional worlds empower people with the tools to transform their own environments. This is what architecture ought to be" (*Dezeen Magazine* 2015).

Besides using LEGO bricks as a way to explore building and architecture, there are other tools you can use as well. ARCKIT is a new model-making kit developed in Ireland that allows you to bring your architecture projects to life. These are not bricks like LEGO, but a variety of components such as panels, floor pieces, and windows that work in a modular fashion for building. You can even print out texture sheets to add details, like wood, stone, or brick, to your completed model. You can also combine these kits with a 3D design program by adding a SketchUp component to your program. SketchUp is a free design program that you can download to your computer to create design for 3D printing, and it is used for a variety of practical applications, including architecture. In the SketchUp 3D Warehouse, you can recreate your ARCKIT designs in a digital format.

Minecraft and Geology

Another great real-world connection to make from Minecraft is to the world of geology. In the game, kids are building, crafting, and creating with a wide variety of materials, many of which are found in the real world. Thousands of kids around the world know what obsidian is thanks to Minecraft. There's a great piece that Geoscience Australia put together called "Geology of Minecraft" (http://www.ga.gov.au/corporate_data/79560/79560.pdf). This is a great place to start a conversation about comparing what you can do with rocks and minerals in Minecraft and what their real-life counterparts can and cannot do. Some of the common rocks and minerals found in Minecraft, besides Obsidian, include diamond, slate, granite, limestone, shale, and more. Rock and mineral kits are easy to come by. You probably already have a nice collection of books on the topic in your library, making for an easy way to get started. Finding a local expert either from a university, science museum, or hobbyist to come in and talk with the kids about geology, rocks, and minerals should not be too difficult either. This is an easy and fun way to bring in STEM and really bring home the "In Real Life" part of the program.

Minecraft and Agriculture

As Minecraft has updated over the years, more and more animals and plants have become part of the game. You can create a garden and grow vegetables, ride horses, and hatch chickens. Instead of doing these things only in the game, why not bring some agriculture programs to your library?

One of the more exciting programs that I've done with kids in the library is hatching butterflies. The kids love checking on the progress and releasing them once they finally hatch. And if that's exciting, hatching chickens at the library would be even more exciting! Local 4-H Clubs have an embryology project that you can sign up for. You can rent the incubator, and receive training and educational materials to run the program at your location. 4-H also runs an Agricultural Literacy Project, which introduces kids to agriculture and life sciences. The program focuses on plant and animal sources of the food we eat, so it is definitely a real-life tie-in to Minecraft.

If plants and gardening are more to your taste, you can bring this kind of program to life in a variety of ways. If you have the space and approval, planting a garden at the library is a great way to bring the game to life for all to see. If that's too ambitious or you don't have the space, you can always plant flowers to liven up your library or have the kids plant flowers in pots to bring home. As part of either kind of program, you can learn about the life cycles of plants and flowers and give the kids a hands-on experience with growing plants for food or decoration.

Minecraft and Music

Minecraft can also be used as a gateway to exploring music, composition, and synthesis. In the game, one can add musical selections to their world by adding a jukebox and collecting music discs. You can even add your own MP3s to Minecraft when playing the PC version of the game by using a resource pack, like you would when adding textures to your world. The jukebox and music discs can be a way to introduce the world of analog music to the kids. With digital downloads, Soundcloud, and streaming services being the way many young people access music today, introduce the old-fashioned jukebox that played 45-inch vinyl records to your club through video or perhaps by an expert in your community. If you have your own vinyl record collection, you could share some of those items with your group. A simple program would be to have the group look at any vinyl records you have to share and making observations about the records. Vinyl records often have interesting cover art, liner notes, sometimes the vinyl itself is colored, and more. The group can talk about the similarities and differences between vinyl and downloading or streaming music, listen to a few tracks, and see a record player in action. You can combine this with an artistic activity such as having the kids create cover art for a Minecraft record.

The second way in which music is found in Minecraft is through special mechanisms called Note Blocks. Note Blocks are powered by Redstone and play a note when you hit them. The instrument that is played by a Note Block is determined by the block it sits on. For example, if you place your note block on top of a wood-based block, you will get a bass guitar, and if you place your note block on a netherrack, you get a bass drum. People have created machines in the game recreating their favorite tunes, note by note. Note Blocks are a great entry point for introducing composition or learning about electronic music creation in the real world.

The littleBits Korg Synth Kit is a great way to get into creating music and learning about synthesizers and electronic music. The Synth Kit is a great entry point to synthesis, allowing you to easily create a modular

Korg MS-20 synthesizer. Parts included in the kit are oscillators, random, a keyboard, micro sequencer, envelope, filter, delay, mix, and of course a speaker. In a program using the Synth Kit, we look at each bit individually and learn about what it does and how it is used by musicians composing music with a synth, and whether it be a physical or digital synthesizer, the concept is the same. The kids are given the opportunity to play with each bit after explanation, and then combine them together to create their own sounds. By working with each part of the synth individually, the kids can really gain an understanding of how each part of the synth works. Like the Note Blocks, each piece works together to create a piece of music or sounds. While the bits have knobs, the concept is much the same, as a change you make with the filter affects the sound that your synth creates. Combining different types of blocks with the Note Block creates a different instrument or sound.

One of the great things about any littleBits kit is the unlimited possibilities for creating. Much like the array of possibilities in Minecraft, you can broaden your creation beyond the Synth Kit itself. You can add on to this program by bringing in other littleBits kits and having them experiment with adding LEDs, triggering sound with a light or motion sensor, and more. Much like you build contraptions using Redstone in Minecraft, you can create contraptions complete with sound using the littleBits.

If you do not have the littleBits kits but have access to iPads, you are in luck! The iPad is a musician-friendly tablet with quite a few apps devoted to music creation, so you should be able to find an app that suits your budget. For music programs, I do bring in a professional sound engineer to run these programs, but with some research and experimentation on your part, you can offer an introduction to music creation using an iPad or the littleBits kit.

Recommended Music Apps for iPads:

- Korg iElectribe ($19.99)—easy to use, intuitive virtual analog beatbox. You can save your creations to SoundCloud
- Korg iMS20 ($29.99)—a recreation of the legendary synthesizer that the Korg littleBits kit is based on. You can save your work on SoundCloud.
- Bebot-Robot Synth ($1.99)—a synth that anyone can learn to play; this is a great place for beginners to start, but is backed by a powerful synth that lets you create and edit your own sounds. You can also connect this app to the GarageBand app to make it even more useful and versatile.

- GarageBand ($4.99)—this app gives you access to touch instruments that sound like their real-life counterpart such as piano, drums, and guitar. You can use this app to record and create. Great for music programs and for podcasting.

There are many more possibilities to explore crafting and other subjects combining Minecraft and real-world activities. As the game grows and introduces new features, the ideas for programming grow with it. I hope you will explore and expand upon the ideas presented here.

REFERENCE

Dezeen Magazine. (January 26, 2015). *Architecture Should Be More Like Minecraft, Says Bjarke Ingels.* http://www.dezeen.com/2015/01/26/architecture-minecraft-bjarke-ingels-big-movie-worldcraft-future-of-storytelling/.

Epilogue

While preparing for the Minecraft to Maker presentation at World Maker Faire in New York in the fall of 2015, the group I was presenting with often talked about the staying power of Minecraft. Are kids still interested? Will they be interested in this a year from now? What does the future hold for the Minecraft phenomenon? As the tent filled up with eager kids, parents, and educators, hungry for more information on using Minecraft as a way to engage learning, it seems obvious that interest not only continues to be there, but also people are hungry for more.

Minecraft in Real Life Club is something that continues to evolve as I learn more about the game, as updates come out adding new creatures and blocks and as I continue to work with the kids who attend the club. The projects presented in this book represent just a small sample of what is possible in a Minecraft-based club, and as you work with kids at your library, you will find inspiration and ideas come to life. As I worked on this project, new ideas kept coming to mind for new projects for the club. Like the game, the possibilities are nearly endless, and as you develop new skills and knowledge, you'll gain the confidence to take on more advanced projects.

This book really came about from a small idea that came to life as the Makerspace at the library came together, as well as my first experience at World Maker Faire. Here, I had the opportunity to introduce the community to tools and technology they may have only heard about, but in order for it to be successful, it really needed something that was going to get people in the door. I once heard someone speaking about starting a Makerspace at their library, and they said that having 3D printers or other technology at the library was a way to get people in the door through word of mouth. You have something that a few people are interested in and excited about and use that to grow your programs. Minecraft in Real Life programming is a perfect way to do this; only Minecraft is something that a lot of people are excited about. Minecraft is the hook that opens the door to introducing a whole world of learning that many may not even be aware of!

You yourself may be new to some of the projects and ideas presented in the preceding chapters. Perhaps, you have never worked with e-textiles or circuits before and you might even be a little uncomfortable introducing these things to your library, but I hope you will take the leap. One thing I have learned from running maker programs in the library these past three years is that you don't have to be an expert; you just need to know the basics. One thing that I love about this type of program is showing the kids that adults don't always have all the answers and that we can take the journey together to find out what they want to know. By not having the solution in your pocket, you are in an even better position to facilitate the program and help guide kids to finding the solution to what they are trying to accomplish through trial and error. It can be hard to not jump in and provide the answer when a kid is struggling to get their project to work, but if you're not sure of the solution yourself, you can't do this. Instead, you can use the knowledge you do have of the basic concepts to ask questions and help guide the learner to finding a solution on their own.

As discussed earlier, Minecraft in Real Life activities are a great way for librarians to offer programming that ties into those important 21st-century skills that kids will need to develop for future success. Learning through doing is a great way to build these skills and you don't need to be an expert to do it. As you can see, it can even be helpful to not have all the answers at your fingertips. One of the things that this type of programming will do is strengthen your facilitation skills, as you are no longer the teacher but merely a guide for the participants. By honing your facilitation skills and by providing a variety of learning opportunities through Minecraft programming, your library will become a leader for creative and innovative programming in the community. Many communities do not have Makerspaces or other organizations offering this type of programming, and if they do, the fees involved to participate can be out of reach for many families. As libraries around the country try to find their way to the future and looking at ways to continue to be relevant, this type of programming offers a perfect opportunity to become a center for out-of-school learning in their community.

While much of the focus of this book has been on the kids, another thing to consider in offering Minecraft in Real Life programming is the appeal of this kind of activity to families. When I started out, the club was really aimed at the kids and I did not really see a place for parents to participate. In fact, I was very hesitant to include adults in the program itself, as past experience has shown me that adults tend to focus on the finished product and lose sight of the process. The learning you are looking to encourage in this programming is focused on the process and not the final product, so it seemed that having the kids dropped off and picked up at the end was a better approach. At first, this is how the club worked, but as time went on and new and unfamiliar tools were introduced, parents wanted to stick around to see what it was all about. The Minecraft in Real Life Club, along with other maker programs at the library, has evolved into family programming. It seems that parents are not only looking to engage their kids in activities that don't revolve passively around screens, but they are also looking for time to bond with their kids.

A recent night at Minecraft in Real Life Club included a group of kids and their parents working together creating stop–motion animation projects using the Minecraft Movie Maker app, mentioned in Chapter 5. As the participants started to work on their projects, parents downloaded the app onto their phones and really started to get excited about the project. Rather than parents trying to take over the project or tell their kids how to complete the project, the parents learned alongside their children. Many of the parents came up to me throughout the program amazed at this cool activity their kids were engaged in and letting me know how much fun they were having. Several parents remarked that we should have a program like this for them!

Through programs, such as those presented in this book, you can clear up some of the mystery surrounding Minecraft. Adults don't always get why the kids are so excited about the game, but through hands-on learning activities, you can open a door to something that can become a family activity.

While one cannot predict the future of Minecraft and the direction that development will go under Microsoft, one thing seems certain—fans are hungry for more and are looking forward to what the future holds. The same is true for Minecraft in Real Life Club. The activities here are just a start to all the possibilities for Minecraft programming and there is much to be learned to expand these activities in new directions. As you can see, I have not covered as much on using Minecraft as a way to introduce coding to kids. I continue to seek out opportunities to learn more and introduce this type of programming to the library, but at this writing, it's just not something that I am comfortable running myself. There is definitely a learning curve to not only gaining "just enough" knowledge to introduce a topic and feeling comfortable doing so.

While I may still not be 100 percent comfortable with all the topics that are introduced in the club, it has been wonderful to watch how the nonexpert approach has helped the kids grow their own confidence approaching projects with different approaches and really taking risks in bringing their projects to life. One boy, in particular, has been a real joy to watch grow his skills and confidence. This boy started attending the club in the spring and has been attending ever since, rarely missing a session. When he first started attending, he was a bit shy and really looked to me to lead the activity and direction of his work. In the beginning, he was hesitant to put in an LED if he wasn't sure it was the exact placement, and would often check in to see if he was "doing it right." With each session he grew in confidence, and he would check in less for direction and more and more to let me know what he was working on or what he was going to try. At one of our most recent sessions, we were working with littleBits from a set of project directions, but always with the caveat that they may explore other ways to create the project or even create their own design if they wish. This boy, while working to create the same final project as the group, took his own approach and worked on his own design to bring it to life. He could see how the project worked, but wanted to come up with his own way of achieving the result. If he got stuck at a certain point, he would consult with me, but instead of expecting me to tell him how to fix it, I was able to guide him through the process. While it may take some time to get there, this is what is possible through this type of program. The kids will take ownership over their projects and guide the direction of the Minecraft programs at your library. As they are exposed to different activities and skills, they will ask for certain projects and activities. They may even present you with their own ideas for future programs.

Like Minecraft, there are endless possibilities for Minecraft in Real Life Activities. Parents and kids are eager to engage in these activities and the library is the perfect place to bring it to life. Let your imagination take over and you can really connect just about any kind of activity, whether it's a low-tech writing activity to cutting-edge technology through 3D Printing, you can bring it to life. Get out there and get making!

Resources

This chapter includes a variety of resources related to the activities and ideas presented in this book. Some of these resources will help you learn more about Minecraft, as well as ideas only touched upon in this book that will help you explore subjects outside the expertise of the author.

BOOKS AND MAGAZINES

These are some of my favorite books on Minecraft, Making, and Informal Learning Spaces.

Minecraft

An Educator's Guide to Using Minecraft in the Classroom: Ideas, Inspiration, and Student Projects for Teachers (October 2014) by Colin Gallagher—This guide focuses on using Minecraft gameplay as a learning tool in a variety of subjects.

Minecraft: The Unlikely Tale of Markus "Notch" Persson and the Game That Changed Everything, 2nd Edition (June 2015) by Daniel Goldberg, Linus Larson, Jennifer Hawkins—If you are looking for a history of Minecraft, this is your best bet. The book is part biography of Marcus Persson, as well as a look at Minecraft from its beginnings to Microsoft's acquisition.

Minecraft Blockopedia (February 2015) by Alex Wiltshire—If you are looking for inspiration for your programs, this is a good place to start.

Minecraft World Magazine—If you are looking for a magazine to add to your collection, look no further than this new monthly magazine for kids. This magazine is out of the United Kingdom, and features articles on gameplay, builds, Minecraft news, and more.

The Parent's Guide to Minecraft (December 2013) by Cori Dusmann—While this guide may be a little dated, it's a good resource for parents to gain understanding on Minecraft's appeal to kids and educate them on the game itself, online safety, and more.

Minecraft—Servers and Coding

Absolute Beginner's Guide to Minecraft Mods Programming, 2nd Edition (October 2015) by Rogers Cadenhead—Learn to create your own Minecraft Mods and learn to program in Java.

Adventures in Minecraft (November 2014) by David Whale and Martin O'Hanlon—This book is for those looking to go beyond gameplay and get started with Python programming.

Minecraft Modding for Kids for Dummies (July 2015) by Sarah Guthals—This book will walk you through learning to create mods using the LearnToMod software.

Minecraft Modding with Forge: A Family-Friendly Guide to Building Fun Mods in Java (April 2015) by Arun Gupta and Aditya Gupta—Learn the basics of Minecraft Forge, Java, and get started creating your own mods.

Learn to Program with Minecraft: Transform Your World with the Power of Python (December 2015) by Craig Richardson—Learn the basics of Python, and then get started with the tools you need to customize your own Minecraft world.

The Ultimate Guide to Minecraft Server (July 2015) by Timothy L. Warner—This guide will walk you through the steps of setting up and running your own Minecraft server.

Maker Resources

The Art of Tinkering: Meet 150 + Makers Working at the Intersection of Art, Science, and Technology (February 2014) by Karen Wilkinson and Mike Petrich—Find inspiration, project ideas, and the theory of tinkering as practiced by the Exploratorium. This is a beautiful book that is sure to get you excited about learning through doing.

Design, Make, Play: Growing the Next Generation of STEM Innovators (March 2013) by Margaret Honey and David E. Kanter—This is a great read on informal learning space outside of schools. Learn about designing your programs and space for learning through doing from some of the innovators in the field.

Getting Started with littleBits: Prototyping and Inventing with Modular Electronics (April 2015) by Ayah Bdeir and Matt Richardson—Learn about electronics and prototyping with little-Bits, including connecting to the cloud and the Arduino bit.

Leo the Maker Prince: Journeys in 3D Printing (December 2013) by Carla Diana—This informational and fun story is a great way to introduce kids to 3D printing and the variety of applications for 3D printing.

Sew Electric: A Collection of Projects That Combine Fabric, Electronics, and Programming (October 2013) by Leah Buechley, Kanjun Qiu, and Sonja de Boer—This guide will walk you through e-textiles projects from the beginner to more advance, one project at a time. This book inspired the Minecraft Torch Book Light project.

Soft Circuits: Crafting e-Puppets with DIY Electronics (The John D. and Catherine T. MacArthur Foundation Series on Digital Learning) (October 2014) by Kylie Peppler, Katie Salen Tekinbas, and Melissa Gresalfi—This is a comprehensive guide to the basics of design thinking in education as well as running workshops in e-textiles. While this title focuses on crafting e-Puppets, the ideas presented here can be adapted to any e-textile program.

3D Printing with Autodesk 123D, Tinkercad, and Makerbot (November 2014) by Lydia Cline—This is a great book that will teach the basics of Tinkercad and Autodesk 123D through a variety of fun projects.

MATERIALS

These are some great resources for purchasing materials for projects, and some offer education discounts to libraries. If you can't find what you are looking for on one of these sites, you can always search Amazon for the supplies you are looking for.

Adafruit Industries—Similar to Sparkfun, this site is a great resource for purchasing materials, learning, and project ideas. https://www.adafruit.com/.

Maker Shed—A one-stop shop for makers, Maker Shed includes everything from 3D printers to kits to Raspberry Pis and more. http://www.makershed.com.

Soldering Sunday—Creators of the Minecraft Circuits in Real Life kits, Soldering Sunday has everything you need to get started with using Minecraft to teach about circuits. Besides the kits, they also offer a variety of kits and components aimed at young makers. Library discounts available on some items. https://solderingsunday.com/shop/.

Spakfun Electronics—This is a great resource not only for purchasing materials for e-textiles projects, but also for tutorials, project ideas, and skill building. Sparkfun offers an educational discount to schools and public libraries. https://www.sparkfun.com/.

MINECRAFT TOYS AND GAMES

There are a variety of Minecraft toys and games that can be used to expand your activities or help you easily get started with projects such as stop–motion animation or even for passive programs in the library. Most of these items are available at retailers such as Target, Wal Mart, and Amazon.

LEGO Minecraft Crafting Box by LEGO—Of all the LEGO Minecraft sets, this is my favorite. There are a variety of bricks to create the eight suggested buildings. Minifigures in this set include Steve, a skeleton, and mooshroom. The Minecraft color-themed blocks and minifigures make this a great choice for LEGO stop–motion animation, passive building programs, and more. You can add additional LEGO sets to your collection to add more possibilities and characters.

Minecraft Card Game by Mattel—This card game for ages 8 and up is based off the game. Players "mine" resources, "craft" items, and have to contend with Creepers and TNT. You could use this for a game design workshop or offer it as part of a gameplay day.

Minecraft Paper Craft Sets by Minecraft—These easy to assemble paper crafts are an easy way to introduce paper crafts, create sets and characters for animation, and more.

Minecraft Stop–Motion Animation Studio by Mattel—This set includes everything you need to get started to create your own stop–motion Minecraft films. The set includes a movie stage and backgrounds, three minifigures, a holder for your phone or tablet, and other accessories. Compatible with the other Minecraft minifigure sets.

PROJECT IDEAS AND TUTORIALS

These are some great sites to help you get started exploring the world of making beyond the projects covered in this book. These are the sites that you will return to time and again to get inspired, learn a new skill, and create your own Minecraft to maker programs.

DIY.org—This is a great site to get ideas for projects for your club. Kids can have their parents sign them up for accounts and you can create a hashtag to link your group's projects. http://diy.org.

Instructables—This is a great site for finding project ideas and sharing projects you have made. Instructables includes projects of all kinds, including food, electronics, costuming, and more. There is even a Minecraft-dedicated channel full of all kinds of Minecraft projects. Librarians can sign up for a free Instructables Pro account, which among other perks allows you to print out PDFs of Instructables for free. In the past, they have offered Build Nights sponsored by companies, such as Dremel, Brown Dog Gadgets, and Silhouette, which you can sign up to participate in and receive free supplies to run the night. http://www.instruc tables.com.

MAKE:—This is the official site of *MAKE:* magazine and a great place to find project ideas and keep up with what's happening in the maker community. You can find reviews of products as well as directions for completing a wide range of projects, which you can search by project type. Projects are rated by difficulty as well as the amount of time it takes to complete. *MAKE:* is part of Maker Media, which includes not only the magazine, but also Maker Faire, Maker Camp, and the Maker Shed.

- *MAKE:*   http://makezine.com
- Maker Faire   http://makerfaire.com
- Maker Camp   http://makercamp.com

Maker ED (Maker Education Initiative)—This organization seeks to empower educators in all types of learning environments to create meaningful maker experiences for youth of all ages and backgrounds. This is a great resource not only for project ideas, but also for information to help you plan, make the case for making with your Board, research, and coming soon, professional development opportunities. If you need ideas or are looking to improve your facilitation skills, this is a great place to start. http://makered.org.

Raspberry Pi in Education—This is the official Raspberry Pi site and a wonderful resource for not only learning about the Raspberry Pi, but also for finding a variety of projects you can incorporate into your programs. The Educator's Edition of the *MagPi* magazine can be found here, as well. http://www.raspberrypi.org/ education.

Sparkfun Tutorials—A variety of projects and resource guides can be found here. This is a great resource for finding tutorials and guides on e-textiles and paper circuit projects. http://learn.spark fun.com/tutorials.

The Tinkering Studio—Part of the Exploratorium, you can find instructions that include tips for facilitating the project in your library. http://tinkering.exploratorium.edu.

Index

About the Author

MARY L. GLENDENING is director of the Middletown Free Library in Media, Pennsylvania. She runs the library's Makerspace, Create-Space@MFL, and founded the library's Minecraft in Real Life Club. She received a Pennsylvania Library Association Best Practices Award in 2014, recognizing the club as one of the best in the state serving school-age children.